I Know Coffee

Harvesting, Blending, Roasting, Brewing, Grinding & Tasting Coffee

By

Jessica Simms

JESSICA SIMSS

I Know Coffee: Harvesting, Blending, Roasting, Brewing, Grinding & Tasting Coffee

Copyright © 2017

All rights reserved. This book or any portion thereof may not be reproduced or used in any manner whatsoever without the express written permission of the publisher except for the use of brief quotations in a book review.

ISBN-10: 1549726048

ISBN-13: 978-1549726040

Warning and Disclaimer

Every effort has been made to make this book as accurate as possible. However, no warranty or fitness is implied. The information provided is on an "as-is" basis. The author and the publisher shall have no liability or responsibility to any person or entity with respect to any loss or damages that arise from the information in this book.

Publisher Contact

books@skinnybottle.com

Introduction to Coffee 1

Harvesting Coffee 5

The Life of a Coffee Bean from Planting to Processing 5

The Journey of the Bean 7

Historical and Botanical Background 9

Cultivars and Varieties 12

Environmental Conditions 18

Farming Methods 23

Coffee Growing Regions 29

Pest Control 40

Plucking and Sorting 44

Processing 47

No Harvest? No Problem! 52

Blending Coffee 53

Your Guide to Coffee Blends and the Perfect Cup 53

More Than a Bean! 55

Understanding Coffee Flavors 57

The Flavor Wheel 64

Regional Profiles 71

The Artful Blend 76

Flavored Coffees 81

Go Blend! 85

Roasting Coffee 87

How to Roast Green Coffee Beans like a Pro 87

Bring out the Beans! 89

Green Coffees 91

Basic Roasting Processes 97

    Roast Levels 103

    Choosing Your Roast 108

    Commercial Roasting... 114

    Home Roasting... 119

    Timing is the Key 128

Brewing and Grinding Coffee 131

    How to Make Good Coffee at Home.. 131

    Mr. Coffee machine.. 133

    Brewing Basics 135

    Grinding Basics.. 140

    Espresso 144

    Drip Brewing.. 151

    Pour Over and Chemex 156

    French Press.. 161

    Other Immersion Brewers 165

    Aeropress... 170

    Cold Brewing... 174

    Other Brewing Methods 179

    It's Up to You.. 183

Tasting Coffee 185

    Coffee Cupping Techniques to Unleash the Bean! 185

    The Idea Behind Coffee Tasting 187

    Supplies for Home Tasting 189

    The Taster's Vocabulary... 195

    Flavor Wheels 199

    Using Flavor Wheels 204

    Identifying Off Flavors 211

Training Your Palate 217
Professional Cupping 221
Home Tasting Practices 227
The Full Picture 231

Jessica Simms is a fiction writer and freelance ghostwriter living in Pittsburgh, PA. In her former life as an SCAA-certified barista, she saw every step of the coffee production process, from picking cherries on a farm in Costa Rica to slinging espresso drinks adorned with latte art to customers at the café. Though she no longer serves coffee professionally, her experiences in the industry have given her a life-long love of the beverage, and she is on a continuous quest for her new favorite bean. Her literary creds include an MFA in creative writing from Chatham University and several short fiction publications in literary journals, most recently Menda City Review, Wraparound South, and Rind Literary Magazine. She is a fiction editor with the After Happy Hour Review and a co-founder of The Haven, a Pittsburgh-based workshop group and literary community.

Introduction to Coffee

Coffee is one of the most popular beverages in the world. Around 145 million bags of coffee are consumed each year worldwide. People in the United States alone consume around 146 billion cups of coffee every year, but when it comes to per capita consumption, the nation doesn't even hit the top, and it is one of the few beverages that is made in some form in nearly every country in the world. Despite its popularity, most people only interact with coffee in its roasted, ready to brew form, and know very little about the growing and processing the plant undergoes to get from the tree to the cup.

The complexity of flavor that makes coffee so popular as a beverage can also make it daunting to get into when you want to learn more about how those flavors are developed. Coffee's flavor comes from a combination of hundreds of compounds that are released from the bean into the cup. No single compound is more important than any other to getting the best taste out of the bean; it is the ratio and interaction of the various compounds that gives coffee its various flavor notes. The type of plant and the conditions that it's grown in will determine the potential flavors of a bean, but how it's processed, roasted, and brewed can have an equally significant impact on the ultimate taste.

To make matters more complicated, there is no single gold standard for the "best" cup of coffee. While there are awards such as the Cup of Excellence that are given to recognize the most flavorful crop of a given year, taste remains a very personal; the expert's favorite coffee might not necessarily be yours. You'll find differences of opinion even within the professional coffee community. Some shops use a dark roast blend for espresso, for example, while others prefer medium- or light-roasted single origins. When it comes to coffee drinks like cappuccinos and lattes, preparation standards can vary greatly from region to region and shop to shop.

This can all be a bit overwhelming for a beginner. While it can take some time and effort to explore the world of coffee, though, the work will ultimately prove rewarding. The more you know about the beans you brew, the better you'll be able to discern just what qualities appeal to you in a cup of joe. Once you're able to make sense of all the countries, cultivars, and roast levels listed on the store shelves, the coffee world will start to seem far less mysterious.

The coffee bean that we know is actually the seed of the plant, which grows inside small round, red fruits known as cherries. The initial processing of the bean is concerned with how the coffee bean is removed from this fruit covering and dried. Even at this point, though, the bean isn't quite ready to brew. It is in what's known as its "green" form, raw seeds that will be soft, dense, and pale—not at all like the hard shiny beans you're used to. If you tried to brew green beans, you'd end up with a cup that's weak, bitter, and thin with a raw, green taste, nothing like the rich, bold beverage that's so popular around the world. A number of chemical and physical changes are brought about during the roasting process that give the beans their distinctive dark brown color and alter the flavor, giving it the distinctive taste coffee is known for.

Coffee will only grow between the Tropic of Cancer and the Tropic of Capricorn, a region of the world that has been nick-named "the coffee belt." This geographic limitation and the agricultural demands of coffee trees mean most hobbyists can't grow their own coffee at home. The rest of the steps of the process, from roasting the beans through grinding and brewing, setting up professional-style tastings, or even steaming milk for lattes and cappuccinos can be done just as well by a home enthusiast as it can by a barista, with the right equipment and a bit of knowledge.

This book is designed to walk you through everything you need to know about coffee from the seed to the cup. It begins with an overview of cultivars and varieties, and the major differences between the three primary coffee-growing regions (Africa, Asia, and the Americas). While there are no hard and fast rules for what coffee from different regions will taste like, it will point out the general characteristics you can expect to find in most coffees grown in a specific area of the world. Though most commercial coffee plants can trace their roots back to just a handful of cuttings, there are today hundreds of different varieties, both man-created and naturally occurring, that have their own typical characteristics, as well. This chapter will also give an explanation of processing and drying methods, and the ways those can impact the bean's development and most prominent flavor notes.

Single-origin coffee is the current trend in artesian coffee shops, and with good reason. By brewing a single-origin bean, you can focus on the distinctive notes that one bean brings to the table. For many, though, the coffee-drinking experience is all about the complexity of the flavors, and blending beans can be very helpful in that regard. Beans can be blended either pre- or post-roasting; the second chapter of this book will walk you through the typical best practices for creating your own blends. Keep in mind that the same bean can taste drastically different, depending on how dark you roast it. The basics of coffee roasting in this book following blending, though you can certainly swap the order in your own process if you'd prefer.

Finally, there's the part of the process that the majority of people have at least a passing familiarity with: the grinding and brewing. These two aspects of the process are inextricably linked, with certain grind sizes working best for certain brewing methods. Each brewing method brings out its own unique characteristics of the bean; similar to roast levels, a bean that's brewed as espresso could have a completely different flavor profile than the same bean brewed using a French press. The book finishes out with how professionals taste coffee, and how you can train your own palate to pick out the distinctive flavor notes.

While this book is arranged linearly, but you don't necessarily have to use it that way. If you'd rather train your palate before you start roasting, for example, you can certainly do so. The idea behind this book is to give anyone the knowledge they need to brew the best cup of coffee—and to understand exactly what that means for your own personal tastes. There is a reason coffee is one of the most popular beverages in the world, and it's not just the caffeine. Its complexity and variety gives you a whole world of flavors to explore as you delve into the science, history, and preparation techniques for this incredible bean.

Harvesting Coffee

The Life of a Coffee Bean from Planting to Processing

JESSICA SIMSS

The Journey of the Bean

Even if you usually go to a coffee shop for your daily cup, you could theoretically do most aspects of coffee preparation yourself at home, whether that's brewing, making your own blends, or even roasting your own green beans. The recent spike in interest in single-origin and other artesian coffees means this is even easier to achieve than it was a few years ago. Even relatively small towns often have at least one coffee shop that focuses on high-quality, single-origin beans, and you can purchase small batches of green beans—and the supplies you need to roast them—very easily online.

The growing and processing of the beans, however, is not something that can be undertaken by a hobbyist. Coffee plants are notoriously finicky; a slight change in the elevation, rainfall, or average temperature in the growing region can have a profound effect on the ultimate taste of the beverage in your cup. Most beans taste their best when grown at high elevations in tropical regions. Even if you could get a coffee tree to grow in a temperate region like Europe or the United States, the payoff would be a long time coming; while a coffee tree can produce beans for several years in healthy conditions, it doesn't usually start to produce its best-tasting beans until it's around 5 years old.

Even though you probably won't be able to start your own coffee nursery at home, learning about the journey a bean takes from the time it's planted until it ends up at the roaster can give you some excellent insights into why certain coffee tastes the way it does, and can help you to make more educated guesses about the flavor notes of a certain cultivar or growing region when you're buying unfamiliar beans, especially if you like to shop online and won't have anyone around that you can ask about the cup profile.

There are a lot of different factors that determine the quality level of the end cup. The genetic make-up of the plant will give it a certain starting quality and flavor potential, which will then be influenced by the environmental conditions during the flowering and fruit production stages of the bean's development, as well as by the farming practices in place and how the bean is processed and stored post-harvest. At each of these stages in the bean's life, the quality potential has to be carefully preserved to give you a good-tasting final cup.

The information that follows in this book will walk you through the life of a coffee bean, from the first moment the plant begins to grow until it's dried at the mill and ready to be shipped to the roaster. By the time you reach the end of this book, you'll have a much deeper understanding of exactly what has to happen to bring you your morning joe—and how farmers make sure the taste is exactly what you're looking for.

Historical and Botanical Background

In botanical terms, a coffee tree is any plant from the family Rubiaceae that produces coffee cherries (and, as a result, coffee beans). There are over 100 known species in this family, and new species are still being discovered on occasion, especially in the more densely forested regions of the Congo basin. Though all of these species are technically coffee plants, they are not all considered to be "true" coffees; that honor is reserved for plants in the genus Psilanthus or Coffea. This is largely a botanical differentiation, based mainly on the structure of the plant's flowers.

Even all the plants that are classified as true coffees are not necessarily suitable for grinding up and brewing into a cup. In fact, of the hundreds of species of coffee plant that exist, only two are regularly used for the preparation of the beverage: Coffea arabica (Arabica coffee) and Coffea canephora (Robusta coffee). Somewhere between 60% and 75% of the world's coffee production consists of Arabica, including the vast majority of coffees you find at your local coffee shop. If your favorite bean is a single origin, odds are good you're drinking an Arabica; even blends tend to be predominantly Arabica, though some espresso blends incorporate Robusta since it can help to create a better crema. While you might hear different plant names being thrown around in regards to coffee like Bourbon or Geisha, these are referring to specific varieties or cultivars of the Arabica plant, not separate species; more information on those specific plants can be found in the next chapter.

Generally speaking, most people find Arabica coffee to have a better, more complex flavor, with a wider variety of potential flavor notes, a smoother texture, and a more pronounced aroma. In comparison, pure Robusta has a tendency to taste flat and doesn't offer the same sensory experience. The main advantage of Robusta over Arabica is its hardiness. It grows better in warmer climates and at lower elevations than Arabica, and is also more resistant to certain diseases that, most notably Coffee Leaf Rust (Hemileia vastatrix), a fungal infection that's a common affliction of plants throughout the coffee growing world. Hybrids of Arabica and Robusta can bring drinkers the best of both worlds, giving you both a complex flavor profile and an enhanced resistance to disease; the best-known hybrid is known as Timor (check out the next chapter for its typical flavor notes and cup profile).

The part of the coffee plant that is processed, roasted, and ground to prepare into a beverage is actually more accurately called a "seed" than a "bean." If you were to look at a coffee tree that's ready for harvesting, you wouldn't see anything that looks like a coffee bean; instead, you'd see clusters of yellow or red berries, known as coffee cherries. The bean used to make coffee is enclosed inside this fruit. There are a variety of ways this seed can be extracted from the fruit (for more information on that, check out chapter 7).

Coffee cultivation: a brief history

The evolutionary history of coffee is somewhat fragmentary. The coffee plant is indigenous to Africa, specifically the equatorial and highland forests of Ethiopia and South Sudan. Wild plants were first noted in the historical record around 850AD, and from there were spread to Yemen and the rest of the Arab world. Africa and the Middle East remained the primary domain of coffee until the early 17th century when European traders drank coffee in the ports of Istanbul and other major cities and decided to take this delicious concoction back to their home countries. A Dutch trader was the first to bring coffee back to Europe in the early

1600s. By 1650, the first coffee house was opened in Italy, and commercial plantations had been started in Indonesia and southeast Asia.

European explorers were also responsible for transporting the first coffee plants to the Americas. Legend has it that every coffee plant currently growing in the Americas is derived from a single clipping that was brought over on a ship from the Netherlands. Whether or not this is true, it is certainly the case that coffee did not exist in the new world until humans brought it over from Africa.

Even though it is not indigenous to the region, coffee plants quickly thrived in the mountains of South and Central America. Because importing beans from Colombia or Costa Rica to the United States is much cheaper and easier than bringing them all the way from Ethiopia, the North American market became dominated by beans grown in this region. Conversely, the European market was dominated by beans grown in southeast Asia, the Middle East, and Africa. This, more than anything, started the divergence between American and European (especially Italian) coffee drinking habits.

Today, coffee is grown in over 50 countries around the world, all of which fall within the inter-tropical belt. Although commercial coffee farms didn't start in the Americas until the 18th century, the land in countries like Brazil, Mexico, and Colombia proved so well-suited to growing coffee that the nations of this region soon dominated the international market, followed by plantations in Indonesia and south-east Asia, with the smallest percentage of the market share coming from Africa and the Middle East—ironically, considering this was where the plant originated in the first place. This is due more to the cultural traditions and farming practices at work in the various regions more than the viability of the climate or soil.

Cultivars and Varieties

All of the beans you can buy in a store or coffee shop come from the two major species of coffee (Coffea arabica and Coffea canephora). Within each species, there are smaller divisions, called varieties, each of which has its own ideal environment and flavor profile. A cultivar is a variety that has been purposefully produced through agricultural means in order to bring out certain characteristics from the parent plants. Most of the characteristics that affect coffee's quality—like bean size, acidity, flavor, and body—are highly heritable, meaning they're passed down consistently from one generation to the next. This means farmers can easily re-create a given cultivar once they've found one that has the qualities they're looking for.

Some cultivars occur in only certain regions of the world, while others are more widespread; some have very specific climate requirements, and others are known for their hardiness and adaptability. Because it's generally regarded to be a better-tasting coffee, the vast majority of cultivars and varieties that are sold as single-origin coffees are from the Arabica branch of the family. The notable exception to this is Timor, a hybrid of Robusta and Arabica that's cross-compatible with either of its parent species. Timor is designed to have the taste of an Arabica along with the disease resistance and productivity of a Robusta and is especially popular in areas prone to coffee leaf rust. It may also be called Arabusta, especially when it's grown in Africa.

The pure Arabica varieties Typica and Bourbon are in many ways the backbone of the modern coffee landscape. Many of the most renowned cultivars in the coffee world are derived from one of these varieties. Both are derived from coffees that first originated in Yemen, although you'll find variants of the Typica and Bourbon everywhere in the world. Typica is known for its high quality, while Bourbon tends to be more productive.

The cultivar gives the coffee bean its potential flavor, which will then be altered and refined by the climate in which the tree is grown and the processing methods. The varieties listed below are some of the best-known in the coffee world. It is by no means a comprehensive list, but will at least give you an idea of the range of varieties that exist.

Heirloom

This is a designation that doesn't necessarily refer to simply one varietal but is worth including in this list because it does tell you something about where the plant came from. There are thousands of coffee varietals growing in Ethiopia. Coffee trees on most Ethiopian farms are able to cross-pollinate more easily than on monoculture farms, meaning that new varieties are always being created. This term has become a catch-all for any Ethiopian plant that hasn't been genetically tested to determine its specific variety.

Caturra

This variety is a mutation of Bourbon. It's named after the town in Brazil where it was originally grown and does best in a similar environment—a medium to high elevation with an annual rainfall of around 100 inches a year. While Bourbon is already a productive plant, Caturra produces even more beans of a more consistent quality, which makes it very popular despite the fact that it requires a lot of hands-on care and fertilization.

Catimor

This is one of the few varieties that has a bit of Robusta in its lineage. Catimor is a cross between Caturra and Timor and was developed to heighten the bean's disease and pest resistance. It has a darker flavor than Caturra, more bitter with fewer sweet notes, but it otherwise has a similar taste profile to Caturra and gives farmers a similar balance of production and quality even when it's grown at lower altitudes.

Mundo Novo

This is a cross between Bourbon and Typica that was first described in the 1940s. It was first grown in Brazil, and if you hear anyone referring to "Brazilian Bourbon coffee," this is probably the variety they mean. It has a relatively high disease resistance and grows best at a medium to low altitude. It has a slow maturation but a high production and can be planted in dense plots, which combines for a dense, flavorful bean that has a high yield. It is more closely related to Sumatra coffee than many American varietals, which gives these beans a more rounded overall flavor.

Geisha

You may remember the hype a few years back about this rare, wonderful coffee that cost about $80 a pound. That particular bean was a geisha, specifically one grown in Panama, and it is considered by some experts to be the best coffee in the world. One of the reasons it's so expensive is that the Geisha must be grown at high altitudes to reach its full potential, which means it has a relatively low yield and there aren't a lot of places that it can thrive. The taste is exquisite, with notes of citrus, jasmine, and honey and a heady, floral aroma, but it's the rarity as much as the quality that drives up the price. This varietal was originally a mutation of Heirloom and grown in Ethiopia. You can find geishas grown in a variety of countries; the ones from Panama are the most prized.

Blue Mountain

The Blue Mountain variety gets its name from the Blue Mountains in Jamaica where it is mainly grown. It's a variant of the Typica variety but with a higher disease resistance and better-suited for growth at high altitudes. The beans grown in Jamaica are in high demand since over 80% of the crops are exported to Japan, making it one of the world's most expensive varieties; the same variety grown elsewhere in the world gives a similar cup flavor but at a significantly lower price. The mild flavor, low acidity, and low bitterness are what make this coffee so admired in terms of taste. When it's grown outside of Jamaica, it may not bear the Blue Mountain name; look for PNG Gold out of Papua New Guinea or Boyo out of Cameroon.

Maragogype

This is a mutation of the Typica variety that was discovered in the Bahia region of Brazil. Maragogype beans are significantly larger, giving them the nickname "Elephant Coffee Beans." The quality of Maragogype depends heavily on the soil in which it was grown. Good Maragogype has a mild flavor with a clean finish and a low acidity; lower-quality beans can have a flat taste and poor aroma.

French Mission

This is a name given to a variety of Bourbon that was planted by French missionaries in Africa, giving it its name. It was first planted in the late 19th century and likely has some Mocha qualities as well from natural mutations that occurred growing alongside beans brought from Yemen. Many of the most prized Kenyan varieties were derived from this bean, notably K7, a version of French Mission grown primarily at the Legetet Estate. French Mission beans tend to have a flavor that's sweet and nutty, with a mild overall cup profile and a smooth texture.

Ruiru 11

Another Kenyan coffee is the Ruiru 11 cultivar, which was developed at Ruiru station in the 1970s. The initial intent was to create a highly resistant strain of coffee by crossing Timor (resistant to leaf rust) and Rume Sudan, a variety with resistance to coffee berry disease. The bit of Robusta added to the mix from the Timor also gives this coffee a high yield, but there is some controversy still about the taste effect on the final cup. Some argue that it is a naturally less complex cup because of its genetic lineage; others insist that inconsistencies in the taste of the bean are caused by a lack of pruning from the farmers, who want to get the highest possible yield out of their crop. The generally held opinion in the professional coffee world is that Ruiru 11 has some of the dry berry notes Bourbon is known for but gives a less flavorful overall cup than other Kenyan varieties.

SL28 and SL34

On the other side of the Kenyan equation are the cultivars SL28 and SL34. Both of these were developed by Scott Labs in the early 20th century. You can identify beans developed by Scott Labs because their name will start with the designation "SL" followed by the number. It's believed up to 90%

of beans currently grown in Kenya were derived from a Scott Labs-developed bean. The 28 and 34 varieties, in particular, have gained quite the reputation among coffee aficionados. SL34 was based on French Mission and has a generally higher yield and can grow at lower altitudes than many Scott Labs cultivars. SL28, meanwhile, is admired for its combination of drought resistance and high cup quality, with a black current-like acidity and a clean overall flavor profile.

Environmental Conditions

As was mentioned in chapter 1, both Arabica and Robusta originate from Africa—specifically the equatorial rainforests in the northern half of the continent. The exact conditions that are ideal for each of these species are different, however. Arabica typically grows best with an average temperature of between 64°F and 70°F, at an elevation of 3,900-6,400 feet and with an annual rainfall of 43-79 inches. It also has specific soil conditions that are most conducive to its growth—typically deep soils that are red or reddish-brown and have good drainage, with a pH of 4.1 to 6.3. In terms of where you'll find these conditions, the ideal agro-ecological zone for Arabica is between around 20° north latitude to around 25° south latitude.

The ideal growing conditions for Robusta are a bit different. Like Arabica, it prefers reddish soils that are well-drained and either flat or have a very gentle slope. Robusta grows best in fairly acidic soil that has a low native fertility. In terms of climate, Robusta likes an average temperature of around 71°F-79°F with an annual rainfall of 47-98 inches, and it prefers a lower elevation than Arabica, somewhere in the neighborhood of 800-4,900 feet. The ideal agro-ecological zone is slightly reduced compared to Arabica, spanning around 15° north to 15° south latitude. As you can see, Arabica is better adapted for cold, while Robusta is better adapted for the heat.

This environmental preference of each of the plants is part of the reason they tend to differ in terms of taste and complexity. In general, the higher the elevation at which the plant is grown, the cooler the conditions and the more slowly the fruit and enclosed bean will mature. A slower maturation process results in a denser bean with a more intense flavor. This has to do with which volatile compounds like acetone and ethanol are allowed to develop within the bean; these are the compounds most responsible for qualities like aroma, acidity, and fruity flavor notes.

Of course, there are not only exceptions to these general ranges of temperature, rainfall, and elevation, but there are also significant variations within the range that can have a major impact on the overall flavor of the cup. Various regions of the coffee growing world have different combinations of soil quality, elevation, rainfall, and temperature. These can generally be grouped into five categories: hot-dry, hot-wet, constant, cool-variable, and cool-dry.

Hot-dry

Around a quarter of the world's commercial coffee comes from a hot, dry region of the world. These regions tend to have a relatively low elevation, around 2,500-3,000 feet, making it a generally better environment for Robusta than Arabica, though there are exceptions to this rule. Hot, dry climates are found in western Africa and regions of Brazil. Beans tend to have a relatively low density and require heavy use of shade to bring out the best flavors.

Hot-wet

Hot and wet climates tend to be found in low to medium elevations, and though less of the world's coffee is grown in these environments than in hot, dry climates, they are found in every major region. As with hot, dry climates, it tends to be a better environment for Robusta and Arabica. It can be found in Central African countries, certain regions of southeast Asia (especially Vietnam), and coastal and island regions throughout Central America. Coffee in these areas tends to be very fast-growing, giving the farms high yields, though the flavor is more subtle and they tend to have less aroma.

Constant

You could say that a constant environment provides the best overall climate for your basic, very good cup of coffee. The beans grown in these environments will not be spectacular, like the coffees grown at very high altitudes, but the trees will strike an excellent balance if yield and flavor. About a quarter of the world's commercial coffee crops are grown in constant environments, the vast majority of which is Arabica.

Constant climates are found in areas like Costa Rica, Colombia, Ethiopia, and Indonesia, where the relatively stable equatorial weather is balanced by the medium to high elevation of the farm. A wide range of different flavors can be brought out of the beans grown in this environment, largely through different farming and processing methods.

Cool-wet

A fifth of the world's coffee comes from a cool, wet environment—including some of the most highly-prized coffees in the world. Cool, wet environments tend to be found at high elevations, and the beans grown in them are dense with a complex flavor, texture, and aroma. Many African nations have a cool, wet environment, including Uganda and Kenya, as do South American nations like Peru and Colombia.

Cool-dry

Also tending to come from higher elevations, the cool, dry environment is the least common among commercial coffee crops, probably in part because coffee grown in this environment has the lowest per-tree yield of any of the different climate zones. Like cool, wet environments, the beans grown here will be very dense and have an intense flavor.

Climate stressors

Even when it's grown in a region known for producing great beans, mother nature doesn't always cooperate by providing the right climate. Coffee farmers have to be able to adapt to weather conditions when they're not ideal. Climate-related stress can be responsible for reduced growth or damage to the leaves, issues with the tree's metabolism, or in extreme cases even tree death.

Excessive high wind can cause damage to the branches and leaves or even strip the leaves completely off the plant. Planting trees around the coffee plants can help to provide windbreaks that will reduce the potential of damage to the coffee trees. Pruning the coffee plants regularly also helps to strengthen the branches, making them less susceptible to damage.

Drought is another common affliction of coffee plantations. Even when it doesn't lead to crop failure, drought can reduce the size of both the trees and the fruit they produce, resulting in a lower yield. Irrigation systems can help prevent both drought and flooding by regulating the flow of water. Temperatures that fall outside the normal range can also impact crops. A higher plant density can be helpful in regions that sometimes experience low temperatures, while regions that can get too hot will benefit from the use of shade trees, which can help regulate the temperature of the coffee trees.

Long-term changes in the climate of a region also have a big impact on the production of coffee trees. In recent years, there has been a trend of elevated temperatures in many of the world's coffee growing regions, especially in the South and Central American nations. This is causing some land previously suitable for coffee growing to become unusable, and is likely a contributing factor to the increased severity of infections like coffee leaf rust in the region. It's uncertain what additional challenges this will present to farmers in the coming years.

Farming Methods

The farming methods in common practice in various areas of the world are determined by a variety of factors, including local cultural traditions, climate conditions, and the topography and condition of the land. Regardless of the specifics of a certain farm's practices, the end goal is the same: to maximize the yield and quality of the beans while minimizing labor and production costs. This can lead to a very interesting pastiche of traditional and modern farming practices in many areas of the world.

Some factors that influence the taste of the final cup are outside of the farmer's control, like the elevation and topography of the land. In most cases, though, there are ways that the farmer can compensate for even unpredictable aspects of the plant's growth, like rainfall or temperature, through the careful management of resources and use of modern farming technology. While each farm's practices will be unique, there are four major aspects that coffee farmers focus on to improve their crops: plant selection, fertilization, shade, and irrigation.

Plant selection

The general category of plant that a farmer will use is by and large determined by the conditions. Certain varieties and cultivars are better suited than others to certain elevations and climates; part of a farmer's job is to choose the plants that will be best able to thrive on his land. Along with choosing which cultivar he wants to plant, a farmer has to select the right propagation system for trees he plants on his land in the future.

There are two general ways that a coffee plant can be reproduced: generative and vegetative. Generative refers to the growth of a plant from a seed and is the easiest and most natural propagation method. It will produce trees with a stronger root structure, but also will take longer for the tree to reach maturity, and is less predictable, with more possible variation from what's expected of the variety.

Vegetative propagation, on the other hand, involves using portions of an already-grown coffee tree to start a new plant, whether that's achieved by planting a cutting or by grafting a branch onto an existing tree. Cuttings are especially useful for large coffee plantations that are hoping to achieve a uniform taste and quality out of an entire crop. They are the best way to produce a new plant that has almost identical taste characteristics to those already on the farm.

Grafting, on the other hand, is more often used to create hybrids between cultivars or varieties. One common practice is to graft Robusta branches onto an Arabica tree to increase the yield or disease resistance without sacrificing the complexity or aroma of the cup. Generally speaking, grafted plants are also hardier and better able to withstand extreme climate conditions like droughts or heat waves. On the negative side of things, they also run the risk of having compatibility issues, which can ultimately cause the grafted branch to fall off of its new tree or even lead to the degradation of the plant as a whole.

Fertilization

One of the key factors in maintaining a successful farm of any kind is to preserve the fertility of the soil. While other crops benefit from rotation, the long lifespan of a coffee tree makes this impractical. Instead, it is up to the farmer to replenish the nutrient level in the soil so that the plants which grow on it will continue to be healthy in the long term.

Several factors determine the fertility of the soil. Some of these are physical, like the texture and depth of the effective soil, or its level of aeration or water infiltration. Others are chemical, like pH, salinity, toxicity, or the ratio of nutrients. Finally, the other creatures that make use of the area will impact the soil. Leaves dropped from other plants, droppings from animals, and microorganisms living in the ground will leave their traces in the soil, which will make their way into the coffee trees.

The most important nutrients for the production of coffee are nitrogen, phosphorus, and potassium, and to a lesser extent calcium, sulfur, and magnesium. Using zinc in the fertilization mix helps to improve bean size consistency and can reduce the instance of coffee berry borer infestation. Finding ways to replenish these nutrients in the soil is important to maintaining the quality of the land and by extension the plants grown on it. Many farmers will regularly sample the soil and analyze its composition to make sure it has the right nutrient balance. This is one-way modern technology can be a great benefit, with both hardware and software available on the market that can make soil analysis easier and more precise.

It's also very important to maintain the right level of acidity in the soil. This is one trait that can have a significant impact on the cup's flavor profile, especially important for bringing out fruity notes. Fertilizers will often have some effect on the pH level of the soil, but there are other compounds that can be used to regulate it, like dolomite, gypsum, and lime.

Shade

Because it evolved in the undergrowth of tropical forests, the coffee tree is naturally shade tolerant. Too much direct exposure to sunlight can bleach nutrients out of the leaves and reduce the complexity of the finished cup, making it bland or even giving it notes of carbon and leather. The traditional arrangement of a coffee farm mimics the environment in a tropical forest, with trees of other species planted between the rows of coffee plants. These not only helped to fertilize the soil by dropping leaves and other organic matter but also provided natural shade.

Starting in the 1970s, large commercial farms started using what was called a full-sun monoculture system, in which the entire plot of land was devoted entirely to coffee trees and the area around them deforested. While this helped to reduce the instance of some insect and fungal pests—especially coffee leaf rust—it also left the coffee plants constantly exposed to direct sunlight.

In the modern era, most farmers find the best tactic to be somewhere in the middle, interspersing designated shade trees in between the rows of coffee plants. A good rule of thumb is around 40% shade cover; any more, and the coffee trees won't get enough heat, reducing the yield of the plants. A mix of species native to the region can also help to keep the soil in its natural balance. By strategically employing shade in this way, farmers can slow down the tree's metabolism, lengthening the ripening process so the flavor in the bean has more time to develop.

Irrigation

Many of the nutrients that end up in the coffee bean are brought in with the water the roots absorb from the soil. Making sure the soil has the right saturation level is important to controlling the rate of the plant's maturation and the ratios of compounds within the bean. Soil that's too wet can also make the trees less stable, loosening the hold of the roots, and can contribute to the proliferation of insects or fungus that can weaken the tree. On the other side, if the soil's too dry the tree will produce smaller fruit and fewer leaves, ultimately resulting in a lowered yield and quality.

Irrigation systems are the easiest way to make sure the water level in the soil stays consistent throughout the growing season. The topography of the region will impact the exact system and arrangement that's used. In cases where the elevation is steep, a terraced system might be the best solution; on flatter lands, systems that run up and down in rows are more common.

Not all farms will need much in the way of irrigation. In wetter climates, the natural rainfall levels may be sufficient to supply the soil with enough water; in these areas, it's ensuring proper draining that's the main concern to farmers. Planting native trees with deep root systems can help to hold the soil in place and keep it from flooding even during heavy rain.

Sustainability

There are some regions in which sustainable and organic farming are almost a given, not because of any regulations of the local government but because farmers in the area either can't afford or don't have access to chemical pesticides and other modern techniques. This is especially true of many African nations, where the long history of coffee cultivation also encourages the use of traditional methods for cultural regions.

Other coffee-growing areas of the world favored a monoculture approach for much of the twentieth century. Farmers would clear the native vegetation completely from the land to make way for the coffee trees, then use an irrigation system to see to soil drainage and chemical fertilizers to return nutrients to the soil. While these techniques can effectively increase a farm's production, they ultimately have a negative impact on the flavor of the coffee. Coffee is one of the few crops that not only can be grown in harmony with its environment but in fact, thrives under a natural rainforest canopy. The trees provide shade for the leaves, slowing the maturation and allowing the beans more time to develop. The roots of large trees also help with soil drainage, while the biomatter dropped by the surrounding plants replenish the nitrogen and other nutrients absorbed by the coffee trees, eliminating the need for costly commercial fertilizers.

While many large plantations in both Indonesia and South America continue to use a monoculture approach, there has been a definite shift in recent years toward a more sustainable approach by smaller farms.

The use of chemical pesticides is a trickier question. Part of the reason the sustainable growing movement has been met with such enthusiasm by coffee farms is because it provides a tangible benefit to their business. Beans grown in a natural environment are generally higher quality, and while the per-acre production may drop, the farmer can also save money on fertilizers and irrigation systems. Commercial pesticides, though costly, are also markedly more effective at preventing devastating insect infestations than any natural method. Considering that some of these infestations can easily wipe out an entire farm, it's understandable that many farmers are reluctant to give up the one proven method of preventing this destruction.

It is yet to be seen how the changing climate in the future will affect these efforts toward more sustainable and organic farming practices. The use of hybrids like Timor or grafts of Robusta onto Arabica plants can improve the resistance of the plants to diseases like coffee leaf rust, and can also help the plants to adapt to warmer temperatures. While coffee purists might object to these practices on a taste basis, it may become more and more common in the coming years as farmers adapt to their changing landscape.

Coffee Growing Regions

There are three general coffee growing regions in the world: Africa, Central and South America, and Southeast Asia. These are broad areas, obviously, between them encompassing over 50 different countries, so you can't necessarily predict how a coffee will taste just because of what continent it comes from. Despite the variations, there are some general traits you can expect from a given region's coffee, mostly due to what varieties, farming technology, and processing methods are available to the farmers.

The sections that follow will give you an overview of what defines the coffees from the world's various regions. Each section starts with a general description of that regions over-arching traits, followed by a more detailed description of the coffees from the most popular or noteworthy countries. As you'll see, some regions and countries show more variation than others, but all have their own distinctive traits and profiles.

South and Central America

Three of the five largest coffee producing countries in terms of pounds sent for export are in this region of the world. Especially for the North American market, it is the region that best exemplifies the "standard" cup of good coffee. Good Latin American coffee is known for having a clean finish and a bright acidity, but there is a lot of variation in cup character depending on the exact nation of origin. High-grown coffees from both Central America and northern South America tend to be bold with a full body. Lower-grown American coffees have a softer, rounder flavor, and can be sweet or dark.

While there are naturally-occurring mutations that have come out of South and Central America—many of which are now popular variations in their own right—the planting of coffee trees on farms in the Americas is very controlled, with the farmer choosing the right cultivar to suit his soil, climate, and elevation. There is also a lot of control on the processing side of things. Though most coffee farms in this region are small, family-owned operations, the majority of Central and South American coffees are wet-processed in centralized mills, which helps to give them their clean and consistent finish.

Brazil

Brazil is the world's largest coffee producer, something that is at least in part due to the extensive geographic area suitable for growing coffee in the country. Brazil is also the most atypical American coffee-growing country in terms of the farming and production of the beans. Coffee farms in Brazil tend to be large plantations which employ hundreds of workers, often with their own on-site processing facilities, which leads to more variation in the bean's flavor. It is also not uncommon for these farms to employ multiple production methods, sometimes within the same harvest, giving the beans even more variation.

Brazil's large area also means a lot of variation in climate throughout the country. Both Arabica and Robusta are grown here, with the farm's elevation largely determining which species of coffee will grow the best in a given area. This diversity of varieties allows for more naturally-occurring mutations in Brazilian coffee farms than elsewhere in the region; many varieties that are now popular elsewhere in the world were first discovered in Brazil.

In general, growing areas in Brazil are at a lower elevation than the rest of the region (around 2,000 to 4,000 feet) which gives them a relatively low acidity and mild, more nuanced overall flavor. The typical profile of a good Brazilian coffee is a sweet, medium-bodied cup with a clear, clean finish. Coffee from the Bahia region is known for its impressively large beans; other popular growing regions are Mogiana, Sul Minas, and Cerrado.

Colombia

The world's second-largest coffee producer, Colombia is arguably the world's best-known coffee-growing region, especially from the perspective of the North American market. Colombia exemplifies American coffee both in terms of process and taste. Beans are grown on small family-owned farms, and there are thousands of these farms throughout the country. The landscape tends to be at a high elevation and very rugged—the perfect environment for coffee growth, though less so for transportation, and even to this day beans are often transported by jeep or even mule out of necessity.

The highest grade of Colombian coffee is called Colombian Supremo. It has a delicate flavor with sweet notes and a high aroma. The second-highest grade, Colombian Excelso, has a similar flavor but with more acidity. Good Colombian coffees are known for their balance more than any specific flavor notes.

Peru

Like Colombian coffee, Peru's coffee farms tend to be small, family-owned, and at relatively high elevations. Most Peruvian coffees are wet-processed, with the best beans coming from the Chanchamayo and Urubamba Valleys. The country employs its own unique grading system for beans; most beans you'll find in specialty shops is of the highest grade, AAA.

You'll often hear Peruvian coffee described as being good for blending because of its understated character. The best beans have a light, mild flavor with sweet, nutty notes, a generally low acidity and light body, and tons of aroma. Lower-quality Peruvian beans are often used as dark roasts or as a base for flavored coffee.

Costa Rica

The largest coffee producer in Central America, Costa Rican coffee is perhaps the most consistent of any nation's. The topography of the region is mountainous, with a high elevation and relatively wet climate. All of Costa Rica's exported beans are wet-processed Arabicas. These are grown on small farms then immediately sent to centralized processing facilities, known as beneficios. While there is some variation in the drying process (you'll find both mechanically- and sun-dried offerings) the rest of the process is relatively consistent across the country. You'll find it has a sharp, bright acidity and a medium body, and the overall cup tends to be well-balanced with notes of chocolate and citrus.

Guatemala

Like Costa Rica, Guatemala has a rugged landscape that provides volcanic soil at high elevations of 4,500 feet or more. This results in a bean that's generally medium or full-bodied with spicy or chocolatey notes and a complex, lingering flavor. Because there are many microclimates in the country, the specifics of the cup will vary region to region. The three main growing regions are Antigua, Coban, and Huehuetenango; you'll see beans from all three on the North American market.

Nicaragua

The late 20th century was a difficult time for Nicaraguan coffee farmers. Not only did the country go through a brutal civil war, Hurricane Mitch ravaged the nation's farmland in the late 1990s. It is only in recent years that Nicaraguan coffees have become widely available again on the export market. The best beans come out of the Jinotega, Matagalpa, and Segovia regions. They're typically grown under shade at high altitudes and have a fragrant complexity, with notes of both nut and chocolate.

Mexico

Though its output is lower than countries like Colombia and Brazil, Mexico still produces more coffee annually than any of the African nations. Despite the high volume they send for export, small farms are still more common than large plantations. Most of the farms are in the southern states, including Veracruz, Oaxaca, and Chiapas, where the topography is very similar to the mountainous terrain of Central American coffee-growing countries.

Coffees from Mexico are generally deeper in flavor than South American coffees, with a sharp finish and a pronounced aroma. This depth of flavor makes them especially well-suited for dark roasts and blends since the taste of the coffee is strong enough to shine through the roast level or added flavors.

Hawaii

The only state of the United States where coffee can grow is Hawaii. There are farms throughout the Hawaiian Islands but the best-known ones are on the big island of Kona, where coffee is grown on the slopes of the Mauna Loa volcano. This black volcanic soil gives these beans a high acidity level, while the tropical clouds provide afternoon shade and frequent rain showers, a combination of environmental conditions that give Hawaiian coffee a rich aroma and body.

Africa

Compared to the control exercised at all stages of the process in Central and South America, coffee from Africa is a much looser when it comes to harvesting and processing methods. You'll find a lot more variation from country to country in terms of how the beans are grown, picked, and dried, from the large estates of Kenya to the wild coffee trees of Ethiopia.

Despite this variation, there is a flavor profile distinctive to coffees from Africa and the Arabian Peninsula. These coffees tend to have very assertive fruit, floral, or wine notes, often emphasized in African coffees that have been natural processed. It is believed to be caused by the composition of the soil, though even coffee experts still aren't completely sure just what it is about the African soil that imparts these notes.

Ethiopia

The birthplace of coffee, Ethiopia is the only country where wild coffee forests remain a prominent harvesting source. It is the largest producer by volume in Africa and the sixth largest worldwide. Ethiopian coffees are among the most distinctive and varied, with a lot of the flavor differences depending on how the picked cherries were processed. Most Ethiopian coffee is grown on small family farms, under shade in interplanted lots and without the use of any chemicals. The exception to this are the larger government-run estates in the southwest of the country.

There are three main regions in Ethiopia: Harar, Sidamo, and Yrgacheffe. Both Sidamo and Yrgacheffe coffees that make it to export are wet-processed, prepared at central washing stations in a similar system to that employed in Costa Rica. The only beans that tend to be dry-processed in this region are small batches intended for local consumption, which tend to be less consistent and a lower overall quality.

The Harar region is slightly different. Beans of all qualities are typically prepared in a natural dry process, giving these beans a slightly fermented aftertaste and a complexity that many aficionados find appealing. Regardless of region, good Ethiopian beans tend to have a full body with assertive fruity or winey notes.

Kenya

Coffees from Kenya are the most widely popular of any of the African varieties. They're known for their sharp acidity, full body, and rich aroma. The country employs its own 10-size grading system, with AA being the largest, and in general maintains tight control over the processing and drying methods, which use the most advanced techniques and are generally very technically sophisticated and export crops are sold in an auction system. The overall result of all these factors is a consistently high-quality product.

Kenyan beans are also consistently high-grown. There are two primary growing regions in the country: on the foothills of Mount Kenya just outside the capital city of Nairobi, and on the slopes of Mount Elgon further south in the country. Most of the beans are grown on small cooperatives, though they may share a centralized processing facility.

Yemen

Though Ethiopia was the first place coffee was grown, Yemen was the country to cultivate it commercially. Farms today use many of the same techniques that were employed hundreds of years ago, with trees grown in small terraced gardens. Because water is relatively scarce, the beans tend to be smaller and more irregular, and are always dry-processed. The resulting taste is deep and rich, which earned the beans the moniker "Mocha," which is most commonly seen today when the bean is used in Mocha-Java blends.

Tanzania

The majority of Tanzanian coffees sold in the United States are peaberries, the genetic mutation that merges the two halves of the coffee seed into one dense bean. Most of the country's beans are grown on the slopes of Mount Kilimanjaro or Mount Meru, near the border with Kenya. The beans have a soft and floral flavor, with a rich acidity. It's graded similar to Kenya, with AA being the highest grade and B the lowest.

Burundi

Burundi is a relative newcomer to the North American coffee market. It uses a similar auction-style export process to Kenya, which means the beans that come out of Burundi are typically of a high quality and sell at a relatively high price point. Most of the beans coming out of Burundi are shade-grown and organic, giving them a bright acidity with floral notes and aroma. They're usually grown on small farms in the north of the country then sent to centralized washing stations for processing.

Uganda

The Robusta variety was originally discovered in Uganda, and this remains the bulk of the country's coffee production. The Robusta grown here is typically dry-processed and is rarely sold as a single-origin variety, instead used by commercial coffee manufacturers as filler in blends. While Uganda remains best-known as the birthplace of Robusta, you can also find a few wet-processed Arabicas from the country. The most admired of these is the Bugisu variety, which is grown on the slopes of Mount Elgon near the Kenyan border and has a similar taste, with wine and fruit notes, though it's a bit rougher in texture.

Southeast Asia

The best-known coffees from this area come from the Malay Archipelago, which is the chain of islands that contains the countries of Indonesia and Papua New Guinea. There is perhaps the most variation in terms of both tastes and processing methods in this region, which can have a bright fruitiness or a deep earthiness depending on the farm it was grown on.

Coffee farms in Southeast Asia take one of two forms: either large estates, which often use the most advanced technology for growing, harvesting, and processing the coffee, or small holdings, which are often more traditional operations. Coffees from smaller farmers will typically have more earthiness and may have a slightly fermented flavor; those from larger estates tend to produce a cleaner cup.

Indonesia

Indonesia is third in total coffee production behind Brazil and Colombia. The country made up of many different islands in the Malay Archipelago, three of which produce the majority of the nation's coffee: Java, Sumatra, and Sulawesi. The beans that come from these three regions is distinct enough that you'll typically see it labeled for its island of origin rather than the country as a whole.

There was a time that Java led the world in coffee production until practically its entire crop was wiped out by coffee leaf rust in the mid-twentieth century. The majority of the land was then re-planted with Robusta because of its high resistance to the disease. More recently, Arabica has made a reappearance on the island, mostly on the eastern side of it. Most of this Arabica is grown on large farms that use the most modern equipment for processing and drying, giving the beans a cleaner profile than other Indonesian coffees, with a taste that's bright, sweet, and fragrant.

Coffee from Sumatra, on the other hand, tends to come from small plots where the trees are grown without shade or pesticides. The processing method is in theory very similar to that used on Java—traditionally a washed or semi-washed coffee—but in practice, the Sumatran process is less consistent, with the beans frequently allowed to ferment for longer before being pulped. This results in a coffee with a very intense and complex flavor, rich in body without being heavy. The best-known regions are in the north of the island and include Linton and Mandheling.

Sulawesi may also be called Celebes or could go by the name Toraja (the indigenous people of the island) or Kalossi (the market town most bean harvests pass through). Most of these beans are grown in the mountains near the port of Ujung Padang. Of the Indonesian coffees, Sulawesi has the most variation. The beans grown on small farms are typically dry-processed and have an earthy, pungent flavor reminiscent of a Sumatra. Those grown on plantations are wet-processed and result in a vibrant, smooth cup more similar to Java. Sulawesi is also known for its aged coffees, which are allowed to sit for a time in the warm, damp climate, a process that lowers the acidity and gives the coffee more body.

Papua New Guinea

Like other beans from the region, coffee grown in Papua New Guinea comes in two distinctive versions: estate-grown coffees that are processed in large facilities and small holder coffees that are processed on-site by the farmers. Both versions tend to be grown organically in similar climates and elevations and are wet-processed, but the estate-grown coffees are generally more consistent, with a vibrant clarity that makes the beans well-suited to a light or medium roast. Variations in the drying and shipping methods can give small holding coffees an earthiness or fermented aftertaste.

Vietnam

You're unlikely to see any coffees from Vietnam on the shelf at your local specialty coffee shop, yet the country is the fourth largest exporter of coffee by volume in the world. The reason you likely haven't heard of Vietnamese coffee is because the majority of the beans grown in the country are Robusta, not Arabica. Vietnam's Robusta tends to have a lower acidity, milder body, and better balance than that grown in other regions of the world. This makes it especially popular for use in blends, especially for use in espresso machines, where the addition of Robusta can help to improve the crema.

Pest Control

One of the primary struggles of any farmer is to prevent insects, fungus, and other life-forms from interfering with their crops. This is as true of a coffee crop as any other, and there are some coffee ailments that can be especially devastating to commercial crops. The leaf rust outbreak of 2013 stretched from Brazil all the way to southern Mexico and caused many small farms in Central America to go out of business. Affected regions reported crop losses of up to 70%, and some regions of Guatemala, Honduras, and El Salvador were forced to declare states of emergency due to the sheer percentage of the population that found themselves out of work as a result. The international coffee market is still seeing elevated prices some four years later as a result of this infection.

There are 16 recognized fungal diseases and 19 recognized insect pests that affect coffee plantations. Because of the prevalence of these various parasites, the majority of coffee farmers use some form of pesticide on their crops to protect their livelihood. A certain amount of pesticide use is permitted even in coffees grown certified Rainforest Alliance or Fair Trade Organic, provided safe application practices are used and the products in question are demonstrated as non-harmful to the surrounding environment. While many people have an automatic aversion to the idea of pesticides, the truth is without them the majority of coffee farms around the world would be unable to exist. Because the coffee bean is enclosed in the fruit when pesticides are applied—and then goes through a lengthy preparation process before even reaching the roaster—the likelihood of any chemical traces making it into your finished cup is practically zero.

Fungal and insect parasitism during the maturation process of the bean is the number one cause of defective beans. Coffee tasters with especially well-trained palates can often taste the specific type of ailment that afflicted the plant when they encounter such defective beans in their brewed cup. Check out the rest of the chapter below for more specific information on the most common coffee parasites and what impact they have on the bean's development and taste.

Insect pests

There are two main ways insects cause damage to a coffee plant: by consuming it or by laying its eggs within the plant. While both of these activities are more likely to be aimed at the leaves and fruits than at the seeds themselves, these attacks can reduce the overall health of the plant, making it more susceptible to other infections and reducing the types and amount of nutrient compounds that are stored within the bean, thereby affecting the flavor.

The main insect pest that does damage the beans themselves is the coffee berry borer (Hypothenemus hampei). The coffee plant is the only host for this species, and it can detect coffee plants from a long distance away. When it finds a host plant, the borer tunnels through the cherry into the bean, where it lays its eggs. The larva damages the structure of the bean as they're eating their way out. The tunnel bored by the adult to lay the eggs also frequently allows the growth of fungus and other microorganism infections. Beans affected by the berry borer have a reduced density and tend to have a fermented or moldy taste in the final cup.

Thanks in large part to the use of pesticides, the infestation level of the coffee berry borer is currently less than 5% worldwide. The use of hybrids and grafts can also increase the resistance of coffee plants to the borer, and these practices are widely utilized in high-risk areas.

While the coffee berry borer is the most pervasive insect pest to affect coffee plantations, it's certainly not the only culprit. Several species of insect are known to feed on or lay their eggs on coffee plants, including Antestia bugs, mealy bugs, and several species of fruit flies. There are also insects that can affect the beans after harvesting. The coffee weevil is the best-known of these; it feeds on beans when they're in storage, making them unsuitable for roasting if the infestation isn't caught and eliminated early enough.

Fungal parasites

Of the 16 recognized fungal coffee diseases, five directly attack the cherries: coffee berry disease, oily spot, pink disease, berry blotch (also called iron spot), and American leaf spot, frequently known by the Spanish name Ojo de Gallo. Berry blotch is the most common of these and contributes to malnourishment in the coffee plant, especially nitrogen deficiencies. Berry blotch is most common during dry periods. It causes an early ripening of the cherry, leading to red lesions on the skin that eventually turn brown and necrotic by the time the fruit matures. It can be reduced by increasing the shade the coffee plant receives; this slows down the plant's metabolism, giving the fungus less opportunity to thrive.

Some fungal infections are specific to a growing region. Coffee berry disease afflicts only African crops. It invades the cherry during the first and second stages of fruit growth, around 4-14 weeks after the plant flowers. The beans themselves are unaffected by mild attacks, which leave a scab tissue (also called "cork tissue") on the surface of the cherry and largely affect only the pulpy tissue of the fruit. A more severe infection is indicated by dark brown spots which will eventually cover the entire surface of the cherry. An infection of this magnitude will affect the development and quality of the bean.

Conversely, American leaf spot is an ailment exclusive to the coffee plants of South and Central America. It tends to occur when the temperature and humidity are consistently higher than average for the region. Its effects can be prevented or mitigated by reducing direct exposure of the plant to sunlight with careful use of shade.

The most damaging fungal infection that can afflict a coffee plant doesn't attack the cherries directly, but rather the leaves. Known as Coffee leaf rust, this infection causes extreme defoliation and shedding, and can eventually lead to the death of the tree itself if left unchecked. If the infection occurs in the first two stages of cherry development, it can cause them to fall from the tree. In later stages, the cherries themselves may be unaffected, but the flavor of the bean will still suffer due to the leeching of minerals and nutrients through the damaged leaves.

A fungal infection of the cherry plant can cause a distinctive off flavor in the finished cup. The infection causes the sugars inside the beans to degrade, often replacing them with fungal metabolites that can give the cup a woody, pulpy flavor or a harsh, astringent feel in the mouth. While fungal growth stops once the humidity of the bean drops below 12%-- meaning it's halted by the drying process—any damage done before this point cannot be reversed and will continue to affect the flavor of the final cup.

Plucking and Sorting

With crops that grow in temperate regions, the seasons dictate the planting and harvesting times. With a crop like coffee, though, that grows in a more tropical environment, the exact number of times a tree is picked over the course of the year and which months are included in the growing season will vary greatly from region to region and even farm to farm.

Coffee cherries go through four stages in the course of their development. In the first stage, the cherries form into small, hard balls. From around week 8 to week 26, they go through stage two, gradually growing and softening though they stay green. In stage three, which lasts from around week 26 to week 32, the cherry ripens, turning first yellow and then red. Following this point, the cherry is considered over-ripe; it darkens to a purplish color before starting to wither and turn black.

In most situations, the goal is to pick the cherries when they're in the third stage of development, without picking any cherries that are still in the first and second stage. Too many under-ripe cherries in the mix can lead to the final cup having a harsh or unpleasant vegetal taste. All the cherries on a tree don't necessarily grow and ripen at exactly the same time. Traditionally, the picking was done by hand, bringing the element of human judgment to the process. The pickers would work through the field on a rotating schedule once the harvest period started, leaving unripe cherries on the tree and coming back for them on the next pass.

The only problem with this is that hand-picking is labor intensive. Using a mechanical picker is a lot faster, especially on a large commercial farm. The problem with mechanical pickers is how to get them to discern between cherries that are ripe and those that aren't. Many farms that use mechanical pickers will also utilize a wet processing method. When the cherries are immersed in tanks of water, the unripe ones will float to the top, allowing them to be skimmed off and maintaining the quality of the beans. Farms can also carefully control the growing conditions of the beans through the use of irrigation and shade to help more of the cherries mature at the same time, leaving fewer that need to be sorted out in processing.

Hand-plucking is still the method of choice on smaller farms throughout the coffee-growing world. It is necessary on many farms at higher elevations, where the slope of the growing land prohibits the use of large machinery. As farming technology progresses, some farms are using a mix of these two methods, equipping their human pickers with specialized hand-held harvesting devices. This allows the harvesters to work more quickly while still applying their human judgment to harvest only the ripest cherries.

Some farms also use a late harvest method. This involves leaving the first cherries to ripen on the branch until they've reached the fourth stage, lessening the chances there will still be under-ripe cherries on the branch around them. This gives the finished cup a distinctive, sweet flavor. It's best used in hot, dry growing regions, where the over-ripe cherries can start to dehydrate while they're still on the tree.

Post-process sorting

Sorting the cherries before they go through any processing and drying can help to weed out immature fruits, but there are some variations in size and quality that can't be seen until the beans are freed from their cherries. Regardless of which processing and drying methods the beans go through, they will typically undergo a round of sorting following the drying.

There are two main goals at play in this final sorting: to sift out defective or low-quality beans and to separate the beans by size. Beans that are different sizes will roast at different times and temperatures; too much variation in bean size will lead to inconsistencies in the roasting stage that can diminish the quality of the final cup. As with the harvesting, sorting can be done either mechanically or by hand, with the mechanical method being quicker and hand-sorting giving more precision.

Farms may also look for specific qualities in the beans as they're sorting them. An example of this would be peaberry varieties. Most coffee beans are split into two halves, but in peaberries, these are fused into a single, round seed. Peaberries are denser than normal beans and if left in with the rest can often burn during roasting, giving the entire batch a carbon flavor if there's too many of them. When they're sorted out on their own, though, many people enjoy peaberry varieties because of the intensity of the flavor.

Processing

As you've seen in the previous chapters, the coffee cherry is intact when it comes off the tree. The seed within has to be extracted from the flesh of the cherry and then dried before it's ready to shop to roasters. The way this is accomplished will put its own stamp on the taste of the finished cup. Beans from the very same crop can taste drastically different depending on whether they're allowed to ferment within the cherry or dried first in the sun. In some locations, coffee farmers are limited by available equipment or the traditions of the region in what processing method they use; in others, farmers have more freedom to choose the processing method they think will bring out the best from the bean.

One factor that limits the kind of processing a farm can undergo is the fact that coffee cherries have to be processed immediately after they're picked. Coffee cherries left to sit for too long will begin to ferment; left to sit long enough, and this can ruin the taste of the coffee beans. Most coffee is not processed on the farm where it is grown but is instead sent to a coffee mill, essentially a plant that often processes the coffee grown on several farms in the area. Because the process has to start quickly, that farmers have to use whatever processing methods are available within quick transportation of their farm, often limiting them to whatever method is most popular in their region.

Controlled fermentation is allowed to happen in some processing methods. Fermentation refers to the naturally-occurring biochemical processes that happen when microorganisms grow in the flesh of the picked coffee cherry. During fermentation, the temperature of the biomatter increases and the pH level drops as bacteria, yeast, and fungus break down the carbohydrates and other materials in the cherry. The trick is making sure the right bacteria are present in the mix so that the fleshy tissue of the fruit is broken down without any mold or harmful bacteria developing on or in the bean.

There are three different processing methods: dry, washed, or semi-washed. Within each of these categories, there are subtle variations in how individual mills prepare their beans. The drying stage can be done in machines, naturally under the sun, or some combination of the two. Each of these decisions will have an impact on the potential flavor of the unprocessed bean.

Dry processed

Also known as "natural processed," in the dry processing method fermentation is prevented entirely through the application of heat. The fruit is dried with the coffee beans still inside, typically by spreading them out in the sun, though it may also be done mechanically. This processing method is most prevalent in areas with a hot, dry climate, where the level of moisture in the beans can be predictably controlled; it is especially common in coffees from north and central Africa, and some of the best-known Ethiopian beans are naturally processed.

The fruit is removed from the beans once they are dried. The beans will still go through another round of drying after the removal of the fruit to make sure the moisture content is low enough for shipping. Naturally processed beans have a sweet, complex flavor with a smooth texture and a heavy body. This method is the best way to preserve the natural flavors of the bean, as the fewest chemical changes will take place inside the bean as a result.

Wash processed

In the washed processing method (also called "wet processed") the fruit and beans are allowed to ferment naturally for 12-24 hours before the fruit is removed from the seed. Typically this involves piling the cherries into large tanks, with or without the addition of water. How much water and how long the cherries are allowed to sit are up to the particular mill and farm; making changes in these areas can allow more control over the development of flavors in the bean. This process loosens the hold of the fruit's flesh on the seed; when the fermentation process is finished, the beans are sent through a machine that removes the fruit from the bean, a process known as pulping, after which the beans are dried.

Underwater fermentation brings out the acidity and aroma of the bean and tends to result in a smoother overall cup. If the process isn't done correctly, however—because of variations in the temperature of the beans or improper aeration, for example—it can give the beans an off flavor that's overly earthy, has a musty or moldy taste, or has a faint medicinal edge.

Semi-wash processed

The final processing method is a mix of the wet and dry methods and is known alternately as pulped natural or honey processed. Semi-washed processing is the newest method. It was first developed in the early 1950s but not widespread as a practice until the 1980s. The mucilage (the fleshy part of the fruit) is either only partially removed or not removed at all, allowing for some fermentation before the beans are dried. This gives it some of the sweeter, smoother notes of a washed coffee but without as much acidity.

Though honey processed is sometimes simply an alternate name for semi-washed, it can also refer to an alternate method where the coffee beans are allowed to dry naturally but in a humid environment. Particularly common in Central America, honey coffee has a high aroma and a rich body. There are three different types of honey processing: yellow honey, red honey, and black honey. In yellow honey, the mucilage is partially removed mechanically before the coffee is sun-dried, a process that takes around 8-10 days. In red honey, 50-75% of the mucilage is retained through the drying process, which lengthens the process to 12-15 days. In black honey, all of the mucilage is left on the bean throughout the drying, a process that can last up to 30 days. Black honey is the most difficult of these processes, requiring frequent mixing and rotation to prevent too much fermentation. In general, the more of the fruit is left on the bean for drying, the sweeter the resultant coffee will be.

Intestinal fermentation

Whereas the processing methods above is all done by humans, from the picking to the drying, intestinal fermentation takes a different approach. There are several animal species that eat coffee cherries as a regular part of their diet, including some species of bird, elephant, and big cats. When they eat the cherries, the seeds pass through the digestive tract, during which process the fruit is entirely cleaned off of the seed. In intestinal fermentation, the scat of these animals is collected and the beans sifted out then washed before finally being dried like normal beans. Intestinal fermentation tends to give the coffee a richer body and a stronger, lingering aftertaste with less acidity overall.

The best-known of the intestinally fermented coffees is called Luwak and is collected from the scat of the Indonesian civet cat. In some cases this is collected from wild cats; in others, they're kept on a farm. Though it first appeared in the late 1940s, it is only in recent years that it's made its way to the western coffee market. The civet cat tends to eat only the sweetest and ripest of the coffee cherries, which also ensures that the beans collected in this way are the best the tree has to offer. It takes around 12-24 hours for the seeds to pass through the animal, a similar time-span to tank fermentation methods.

Drying methods

Once the beans have been removed from the fruit, they must then be allowed to dry until the remaining moisture in the bean is between 10% and 12% to prevent mold or fungus from growing during the storage and transportation of the coffee. This drying can be accomplished one of two ways, either mechanically in large dryers or by laying out in the sun. Machine drying is a quicker process, taking only a few hours as opposed to the multiple days it takes to sun dry, but sun drying allows more of the fruity notes and natural sweetness of the bean to develop, resulting in a generally more enjoyable cup.

If the drying is not done correctly it can have a significant impact on the taste of the coffee. Drying too quickly can give the coffee a flat taste; drying too slowly, or not enough, and it can pick up a moldy or fermented flavor. Ventilation and air circulation are key in the drying process, especially for sun drying. Proper rotation of the beans ensures they all dry at the same rate and no damp spots are left once the process is over. If this process is done correctly, unroasted coffee beans can last for six months to a year when stored in a cool, dry environment.

No Harvest? No Problem!

One of the reasons that coffee flavor is so complex is that it is influenced by such a wide variety of factors. While you may not be able to start your own coffee farm in your backyard, understanding what makes coffee taste the way it does can help you make more informed decisions when you're trying out a new roast or formulating blends.

New cultivars are being developed all the time that bring unique flavors, textures, and aromas to the coffee world. If you want to stay up on the current trends, check out the Cup of Excellence winners from the past year, or check out the Specialty Coffee Association of America's website; they often have information and resources posted there that can be of great interest to coffee professionals and hobbyists alike.

Knowing what climate conditions can impact your coffee's flavor is also helpful when you're shopping for beans. If you know it's been a warmer year than usual in Mexico, you can expect the coffee from that harvest to taste a bit different than it normally does. Whether or not you want to get into things to that level of depth is up to you, of course. At the very least, understanding the harvest process will give you a deeper appreciation for how much work goes into your daily cup.

Blending Coffee

Your Guide to Coffee Blends and the Perfect Cup

JESSICA SIMSS

More Than a Bean!

To say that coffee is a bean is a bit of a misnomer. If you were to see a ripe coffee plant, you would find it covered in red berries; the part of the plant that is roasted, ground, and brewed into the beverage is the seed inside this fruit. Coffee trees can grow in a wide range of climates and elevations but they're predominantly grown in three regions of the world: Central and South America, Africa, and southeast Asia.

If all the beans in a bag of coffee come from the same growing region, it's known as a single-origin coffee. You'll typically see these labeled with a geographic name, like Guatemala Antigua or Ethiopia Yirgacheffe. They could also be named for their cultivar, especially if it's a particularly coveted one (e.g. Panama Geisha), or for the farm where they were grown. Because the flavor of coffee is greatly influenced by environmental factors like soil composition, elevation, and climate conditions, knowing where the beans were grown is often a good indication of its flavor notes and overall quality.

If the coffees in the bag come from a lot of different places, it's known as a blend. Some people have the misconception that blends are inherently lower in quality than single-origin coffees. Blends can be used to hide the flavor of inferior beans, but more often they're a way to add complexity to the final cup by pairing complementary flavors. Making your own blends at home can be a great way to customize your daily cup without investing in costly new equipment like a home roaster or espresso machine. While you'll get the most flavor from buying whole beans and grinding them yourself at home, you can also blend pre-ground coffee if you lack the necessary equipment (and the budget to obtain it).

In the not too distant past, the coffee section of most grocery stores was stocked almost exclusively by blends, most of them pre-ground. While this is changing, your best bet for finding a wide variety of single-origin coffees is still likely to be a café or roaster. The staff in these establishments works with coffee day in and day out, and they can answer any questions you have about their beans or point out roasts that seem suited to your tastes. When buying at the supermarket (or from the internet), your knowledge is often limited to what's printed on the package.

The main thing you need if you want to make your own blends is knowledge about coffee—how it develops its distinctive flavors, how to identify flavor notes, and how to figure out which beans will complement each other. The chapters that follow in this book will get you up to speed on everything you need to know to start making your own coffee blends at home.

Understanding Coffee Flavors

There are a lot of different factors that can influence the taste of the coffee in your cup, one of the main reasons it can seem so complicated to someone just getting into the intricacies of the beverage. Every stage of the process from planting to roasting leaves its mark on the flavor of the final brew. Depending on how it's grown, processed, and roasted, coffee can have a bright, citrusy flavor or a darker chocolatey or nutty taste; its texture can be sharp like tea or lingering and syrupy. The fact that so much variation is possible is what makes coffee blending such a complex and fascinating art.

Understanding just what gives certain coffees their distinctive flavor profiles is the first step toward mastering the art of blending. It lets you make informed decisions about which beans and roast levels will complement each other. There are three basic stages to a coffee bean's development: the growth, the processing, and the roasting. Each of these stages is explored in more depth in the sections that follow.

Planting and growth

The first choice a coffee farmer makes is what varietal of the coffee tree to plant. Two families of the coffee plant make up the majority of the beans available on the market: arabica (Coffea arabica), which makes up around

75% of the world's coffee crops; and robusta (Coffea canephora), which accounts for around 20% of them. Arabica coffees generally have a more complex flavor, and pretty much any single-origin coffee you encounter will be arabica. Robusta, on the other hand, is a hardier plant. It's more resistant to disease and variations in climate or elevation, making it a popular component in commercial blends. In a specialty coffee shop, you may see robusta utilized as one ingredient in an espresso blend.

Within the arabica family, there are dozens of what are called cultivars, or cultivated varieties, which you can think of as being similar to the varietals of wine grapes. The same cultivar could still taste drastically different depending on the growing conditions, but which cultivar the beans are grown from determines what range of flavors is possible.

The elevation at which the coffee tree is grown is arguably the most important factor in the developing the taste of the bean. Arabica coffees can grow at a wide range of elevations, from around 1,800 feet to around 6,300 feet above sea level; generally speaking, the higher-grown the coffee, the better the quality. Robusta can grow at a lower elevation, around 600 to 2,400 feet above sea level. The climate tends to be cooler in higher elevations; combined with the lower oxygen levels in the air, this makes the coffee trees grow more slowly at higher elevations, resulting in a smaller, denser bean (sometimes called "hard beans").

A coffee grown at a higher altitude is likely to be more acidic and aromatic, with more complexity in the cup. Coffee grown at lower elevations will be flatter overall, with less acidity and fewer flavor notes, making them good as a background presence in a blend. The fact that these beans grow more slowly also means that the yield per plant tends to be lower, which perhaps even more than the improved flavor tends to make them more expensive.

As a general rule of thumb, coffees grown at certain elevations will have certain specific flavor notes. Those grown at a very low elevation (2,500 feet above sea level or lower) tend to have a somewhat bland taste that may have earthy notes. Those grown at a low elevation (2,500-3,000 feet) are a bit more complex but still have a subtle, mild flavor. Medium-grown coffees (3,000-4,000 feet) tend to taste sweet and have a relatively low acidity. High-grown coffees (4,000-5,000 feet) have a slightly higher acidity that may give them a sweet citrus taste, though they often also have sweet vanilla notes or deep nutty tones, resulting in an often complex final cup. The most prized coffees, those grown at very high elevations (5,000 feet and higher) tend to have the highest acidity and can give you notes ranging from fruity to floral to spicy or wine-like, depending on what's done to the bean after it's picked.

While low-grown coffee is often seen as lower-quality, there are always exceptions to every rule. Coffee from the Kona district of Hawaii, for example, can't be grown at elevations over 2,000 feet; the island is far enough north of the equator that the climate is too cold at higher altitudes. Kona coffee is prized for its soft sweetness and low acidity, but the low density of the beans means it has to be handled carefully and can easily be ruined through over-roasting.

While the climate often goes hand in hand with the elevation, it also has its own influences on the taste of the bean. Especially important is whether the coffee is grown in shade or direct sunlight. In warmer regions, coffee plants can burn if exposed to too much direct sunlight, giving the beans a bitter aftertaste and flatter overall profile. Shade-grown coffee develops more slowly, giving it more complexity. The climate also affects the length of the growing season and at what point in the year the fruit is at its ideal ripeness. Even minor changes in temperature and rainfall levels can have a big impact on the quality of the beans.

The contents and quality of the soil also affect the bean. Not only will the correct ratio of minerals and nutrients encourage healthy growth of the plant but the minerals absorbed through the root will affect which oils and compounds are most prominent in the fruit and seeds. The same cultivar grown at the same elevation would taste very different if grown in an acidic soil, like one based on volcanic rock, than it would if grown in a more basic soil of limestone or clay.

These natural variations in climate, altitude and soil contents are also affected by the techniques the farmer uses to grow his plants. Farms in Central and South America are likely to prune their trees more regularly and use systems of irrigation and fertilization to encourage growth. Indonesian farms don't tend to prune their trees as regularly, and in certain regions of Africa, coffee beans are still harvested from wild-grown trees that undergo no cultivation at all. The more cultivation is employed, the more consistent the beans from that farm will generally be.

How much of this information you have about a particular bean will likely depend on where you shop. A coffee shop that roasts in-house is likely to at least be able to at least tell you which farm the beans came from, including its elevation and typical climate, as well as the bean's cultivar. As you get more familiar with different popular regions, you'll likely start to see patterns and trends in the taste profiles of beans from these areas.

Harvesting and processing

When coffee beans are harvested, the entire cherry is plucked from the tree. A variety of methods are then used to extract the seed from the fruit; the seed is then dried and sent away for roasting. Even on the same tree, the cherries will reach peak ripeness at different points throughout the growing season. Larger commercial farms often use mechanical harvesters, which can't tell the difference between a ripe and an unripe cherry. Since the oils in these seeds haven't been fully developed, coffee brewed from them will taste thin and weak; if they're not sorted out before processing they'll impact the overall quality of the final cup.

Even beyond picking out the unripe beans, how the coffee is sorted has an impact on the quality of the final cup. Both the coffee cherries and the beans inside them can vary in size, even if they grow on the same bush. This can lead to inconsistencies in the roasting if they're not separated by size. This can be done either mechanically or by hand; hand-sorting is more thorough, but machine sorting is more cost-efficient. One thing sorters look for are peaberry beans. This is a mutation found in a variety of different cultivars, in which the two halves of the coffee bean fuse together into one round seed. Peaberries are both smaller and denser than normal beans, which can lead to them getting charred if they're left in with beans of other sizes. When they're sorted out, however, peaberries are often considered to be of a higher quality than normal beans of the same cultivar, with a higher density that leads to better-developed flavors.

There are three main methods for processing coffee beans: dry or natural, wet-processed or washed, and pulp natural or semi-washed. The dry method is traditional and is in the modern industry used mostly by smaller farms. In this method, the whole cherries are spread out to dry in the sun for between 7 and 10 days. The cherry's skin and mucilage will become dry and brittle through this process, at which point they can be removed from the bean. Dry processed coffees tend to have a thicker body and a lower acidity. This processing method tends to bring out both rich fruity and earthy flavors.

A wet-processed or washed coffee is more common in areas that get high levels of annual rainfall. The picked cherries are put into vats full of water where they're left overnight to soften. These softened cherries are then run through pulping machines that remove most of the mucilage before being poured back into water vats and allowed to ferment. The beans are washed of any remaining traces of the fruit and dried either in the natural sunlight or in mechanical dryers. The taste of washed coffees is generally cleaner and brighter than that of natural coffees, with a lighter body and a sharper acidity.

The third processing style, semi-washed, is a hybrid between the dry and wet methods. The cherries are softened in vats like washed coffees but are then sent straight to the drying phase instead of going through the additional steps of pulping and fermentation. Some people find the semi-washed process gives the beans the best of both worlds, with a slightly cleaner profile than a natural coffee that has a bit more body than a fully washed.

Roasting

The inside of the coffee bean undergoes chemical changes during the roasting process that drastically affect its flavor. The sugars in the bean are caramelized; acids that were buried deep inside the bean are brought to the surface. How many of these changes the bean is allowed to undergo will determine the ultimate taste profile.

Beans that aren't roasted are called "green." If you tried to brew green coffee beans, you'd get a beverage that's sharp and vegetal, with bitter undertones like an over-brewed green tea. The roasting process is instrumental to bringing out the flavors we associate with coffee.

The lightest drinkable roast level is a cinnamon roast, named for the color of the beans at this level, not because the taste will have any traces of cinnamon. These roasts will have the highest acidity and a relatively weak body. The step above this is called a light roast or New England roast. It will be more aromatic and complex than the same bean at a cinnamon roast; the majority of beans need to be roasted at least to this level.

The next darkest is the medium or "American roast," so-named because of its popularity in North America. This is the level at which many beans are at their peak complexity, where the flavor oils have been fully extracted but the acids haven't burned off too much.

Finally, there are the dark roasts. The border between medium and dark roasts can be loosely drawn at the point where more than half the acids of the bean have burned off, replaced by a pungent, dark flavor and a fuller body. The lightest is called a full roast or Vienna roast and it is the level at which many beans are at their most aromatic. Next is the French roast, which is also called espresso roast because this is the level at which many beans are best-suited to that brewing method. The darkest roast is the Italian roast. It is the least acidic with the thickest body but with less complexity and aroma.

There are some beans that will taste good at a variety of roast levels, while others are more finicky and best-suited to a particular style. Beyond the accepted standards of the industry, roast level is in many ways a personal preference. Those who grew up drinking American-style coffee may find darker roast levels too pungent or bitter, while those accustomed to espresso would find a light roast thin and weak. Determining which roast level you prefer can help you choose your coffees as you're working on your ideal blend.

The Flavor Wheel

The Coffee Taster's Flavor Wheel was developed by the Specialty Coffee Association of America in 1995 to give coffee professionals a shared language for talking about the various tastes and textures of coffee, in the same way sommeliers talk about the taste and texture of wine. It has since become one of the most iconic resources for the coffee industry, helping both professionals and home enthusiasts to better identify the tastes in their brewed cup. If you're trying to fit the flavors of various beans together in a blend, the flavor wheel can help you to better identify the notes you're tasting, and which beans will complement each other the best.

The flavor wheel was updated in 2016, expanding the flavor options to be better-suited to the modern coffee market. If you're interested in seeing the wheel, you can look it up very easily on the internet, though you'll likely also find lots of variations as many coffee roasters will tweak the wheel to be better suited to their own roasts.

Not everyone's taste buds will be able to pick out the subtle notes in coffee without a little bit of work. Developing your palate is a skill, and like any skill it takes practice. You can do this not only by being mindful when you drink coffee, but also when you're eating other foods. Focusing on the taste of an apple or chocolate bar while you're eating it will help you to then identify those flavors in other things, whether that's a glass of wine or a cup of coffee. Don't only note how the object tastes; also pay attention to its texture and the way it feels in your mouth as you're eating it, internalizing the entire eating experience.

Coffee is a multi-sensory experience. You should pay as much attention to the smell of the coffee and the way it feels in your mouth as you do to the taste. When you're looking for the notes in the coffee, start by smelling the grounds. They'll be at their most aromatic immediately after they're ground, so if you can, it's best to grind the beans at home. You should also smell the brewed coffee as you're pouring it into your cup. At first, it may be hard to smell anything but just "coffee," but search for other aromas you recognize.

Some of the descriptors on the flavor wheel are pure tastes, and others are pure aromatics, but most of the items on the flavor wheel are produced through a mix of taste and smell sensations. Smell the steam of the coffee as you're taking a sip. Once it's cool enough, hold the coffee in your mouth and consider how it feels—if it seems to coat your mouth and linger after you swallow or if it's cleaner and more ephemeral. You could use terms like velvety, smooth, sharp, or dry to describe the feel. Words like pungent, tart and syrupy also describe some element of the feel, though they're also associated with a taste.

There is no one perfect cup of coffee. While there are some cultivars that most people consider to be superior to others, taste is ultimately a personal matter. As you taste your coffee with the flavor wheel, identify which notes you find the most appealing, and which you find particularly distasteful. Eventually, you'll be able to pick out which coffees you'll probably like, or which will go well together, simply by looking at the most prominent notes, rather than having to always find the right matches through trial and error.

Using the wheel

The flavor wheel is designed for you to be able to start from broad flavor categories and gradually pinpoint a more specific flavor. In the center ring, you'll see nine categories: floral, fruity, nutty, roasted, sour, spicy, sweet, vegetative, and other. Each of these categories is typically given a color association that can help you differentiate them, but these are not standardized and you can feel free to change them if another color seems more representative of the flavor to you.

Once you've located the basic category of the taste, move to the next ring, which gives you slightly more specific descriptors. From there, move to the third ring if you can. When you're first developing your palate, you might not be able to immediately pick out anything beyond the first ring. If you're having trouble, use the descriptors in the middle ring and work backward. For example, say you taste some fruitiness but can't tell if it's berry or melon. Imagine the taste of a blueberry and take another sip of the coffee, searching for that flavor. As your palate is further developed, you'll be able to skip this step.

You'll probably find it helpful to keep a tasting notebook while you're doing this so you don't forget what flavors you've tasted when you come back to the coffee to make a blend. You also don't have to limit yourself to the flavors included on the wheel. If you detect notes of mango or green tea, write those down. Each palate is different, and you want to note down what you taste, not what the coffee is supposed to taste like.

Floral flavors

Floral flavors tend to be fairly delicate and subtle, and in a coffee context, you're most likely to find them in lighter roasts. They're also more common in wet processed coffees, which have a cleaner, clearer flavor. Popular beans that tend to have fruity notes include Ethiopia Yirgacheffe and Guatemala Huehuetenango.

Florals are generally found more in the aroma of the coffee than the taste. Examples on the wheel include chamomile, rose, and jasmine. A black tea flavor is also considered to be floral since it often has a perfumey taste.

Fruity flavors

Fruity notes are some of the most commonly tasted in coffees from all around the world—which makes sense, considering the beans are the seeds of berries. Coffees that are dry-processed tend to be fruitier than washed or semi-washed coffees. You're also more likely to taste fruity notes in light roasts than in medium or dark roasts, and they also may be brought out more effectively by certain brewing methods; citrus notes are common in espresso, for example.

The fruity section of the flavor wheel is further broken down into the categories of berry, dried fruit, and citrus, with a catch-all "other" category for other flavors like coconut or apple; some flavor wheels also include the categories of stonefruit (such as plum or cherry) and melon. Light-roasted Ethiopians are known for their berry flavor, while Central American coffee—especially beans from Nicaragua—have a bright, clean citrus.

Nutty flavors

Included in this category are both nut flavors (like hazelnut, almond, or peanuts) and cocoa flavors. Both of these sub-categories are fairly common and are often more pronounced in medium and dark roasts. Milk chocolate flavors tend to have a smooth, velvety texture, while dark chocolate notes are often more bitter. If you're a particular fan of these kinds of notes in your coffee, check out beans from Mexico or Brazil.

Roasted flavors

As you might expect, roasted flavors are most common in dark roasts. Tastes are also included in this category if they have a toasted or smoky flavor. For some, flavors out of this category are too acrid or bitter; for others, a bit of a burnt taste is appealing, especially when complemented by a bright citrus or sweet caramel note. Subdivisions of this category include tobacco, malt, or grain tastes, as well as smoky or ashy notes.

Sour flavors

There are a couple different types of tastes included under the general umbrella of "sour." The first are the tart, pucker-inducing tastes that you probably initially think of. These tastes on the flavor wheel are noted as different kinds of acid, which is generally unhelpful for the casual taster. You may find it more helpful to associate this kind of sour with how it feels on your tongue—whether it's rough or dry or a bit sweet, like an orange.

You can also find fermented flavors under sour, which includes good tastes like wine and whiskey and undesirable tastes, which can indicate the coffee cherries were over-ripe or over-fermented. Sour tastes are fairly common in light-roasted and high-grown coffees from around the world, but well-fermented tastes are less common. Many coffees from Yemen have winey notes if that's a taste you're looking for.

Spice flavors

Spices like cinnamon and nutmeg make excellent complements to the taste of coffee, and you can sometimes also find these notes in the beans themselves. Some beans also have notes of clove, anise, or even black pepper, flavors that are often described as dark, warm, or pungent. These notes can be brought out through darker roasting but can be present in lighter roasts, as well. Beans from the Antigua region of Guatemala are often spicy, as are some Sulawesi beans.

Sweet flavors

As the coffee bean roasts, the sugars within it caramelize. This often gives medium and dark roasts a sweet taste, one that can either be light like honey or deep like brown sugar or molasses. Similar flavors like maple syrup or vanilla are also included in this category. If you're considering textures, you may find these coffees syrupy or viscous. When in a blend, they can provide depth for light fruity flavors, or balance out spicy and sour notes.

Vegetative flavors

This category can be a bit more difficult to describe to someone who's new to coffee tasting. Like sour, it is in part about the feel of the beverage, in addition to the taste. Also, like the sour category, it can include some flavors most people would consider unappealing. This includes a raw or under-ripe flavor, which can come from beans that are either picked too early or not roasted long enough.

If it helps, you could also think of this as the "green" category, where you find herbal flavors along with other vegetable flavors. Coffees that have a beany or pea-like taste would be called vegetal. Good "green" tastes are relatively rare in coffee, though you may detect them in some Indonesian coffees, especially those from Sumatra, as well as in some varieties from Kenya and Rwanda.

Other flavors

The catch-all category on the flavor wheel is where you'll find a lot of undesirable tastes. These include papery or cardboard flavors and tastes that are musty, dusty, moldy, or stale. The chemical sub-category includes bitter, salty, or medicinal notes. While some coffees have a pleasant woodiness or earthiness, like many Indonesian coffees, in general, the tastes in this category are considered to be roasting defects.

Regional Profiles

While some single-origin coffees are named for their cultivar—especially when that cultivar is particularly rare or prized—the majority will have more geographical labels, including the nation of origin and the specific farm or region where it was grown. All the factors discussed in the first chapter play a part in determining the specific characteristics of these different regions. While there will always be situational variations, beans from a given area will tend to grow at a similar elevation and with similar soil and climate conditions; farmers working in these regions will often employ similar techniques for growing, harvesting, and processing.

There are three primary coffee growing regions in the world: Africa, Southeast Asia, and Central and South America. These are obviously very broad areas, and you'll find a huge amount of variety within each region's production. All three areas produce very high-altitude coffee that's highly-touted by coffee professionals. Twenty years ago the vast majority of coffee that could be found in North America was produced in Central America or Colombia, but today Indonesian and African coffees are widely available in most regions of the United States and Canada.

The Americas

Over half of the world's coffee comes from the Americas. There are coffee farms in every nation of Central America, as well as Mexico and many islands of the Caribbean. In South America, Colombia, Brazil, and Peru are the major coffee producers. A lot of the cultivars grown in these regions are based on Bourbon, a cultivar that was developed in the Americas from the first coffee plant brought to the Americas from Ethiopia. It tends to produce beans that are mellow and sweet with a buttery mouth feel. Other cultivars derived from Bourbon include Caturra, Catuai, and Icatu; all three are found throughout Central America.

All the countries in the coffee-growing region of the Americas share a similar climate and grow their plants at a similar altitude. They also use similar processing techniques. Though the soil differs from region to region and the acid content of the beans can vary, you can usually describe American coffees as well-balanced and make a great base on which to build your blends. The highest-altitude American coffees come from Colombia and Guatemala.

Coffees grown in Mexico, El Salvador, Panama, and Nicaragua tend to do best a lighter roast levels. All have a relatively light body with a mild acidity. Mexican coffees, in particular, are known for their milk chocolate notes, while Nicaraguan and Salvadoran coffee tends to have more fruity and vanilla notes. Coffees from Guatemala and Costa Rica have a bit more body and do well at a variety of roast levels. The Antigua region of Guatemala is known for having a spicy, almost smoky quality at darker roasts, while the beans from the Huehuetenango region are more delicate and floral.

Colombian coffee is similar to most Central American varieties. It's mellow and sweet, with a nutty finish, and has a moderate acidity. Coffee from Peru tends to be grown at very high altitudes and in a relatively acidic soil, making it bright and sourer than most coffees. It can be a useful ingredient in a blend if you want to add more high notes to the flavor profile. Look for the Maragogype cultivar for a slightly darker cup, or the

Pacamara—a mix of Maragogype with Bourbon—for a brighter taste. You'll find the most national variation in coffees from different regions of Brazil, where there's a broader range of elevations and a wider variety of common farming practices. Naturally processed Brazilian beans are great in espresso blends because they have a tendency to linger in your mouth with creamy notes of chocolate.

Finally, there's the coffee of the Caribbean. Because they're island nations—and therefore relatively short on space—you won't find as many of these beans available on a regular basis, and the ones you do find are often expensive. Because of that, most people prefer to enjoy them as-is instead of mixing them into a blend.

Africa

Coffee originated in Africa. The plants grown today in the Americas and Asia are all derived from plants that originated in Ethiopia, which is one of the few places in the world you can find wild-growing coffee plants. The highest grown coffees out of Africa come from Ethiopia and Kenya, but you may also see beans grown in Burundi, Rwanda, Tanzania, Uganda, Yemen, and Zimbabwe. This is a large geographic area, meaning African coffees as a category don't have a general taste profile; instead, each country tends to have its own defining attributes, brought about by the nation's specific climate and typical processing methods.

There are a variety of processing methods used in Ethiopia, and while most of the coffee that's exported from this country is grown on farms, some crops are still harvested from wild-grown plants. The Heirloom cultivar is genetically closer to wild-grown plants than any other cultivated variety of coffee and grows predominantly in Ethiopia. Dry processed Ethiopians tend to have a syrupy body with lots of bright berry or sweet winey notes. Harar is a popular dry processed Ethiopian. Depending on the roast level, it can either have prominent blueberry notes or a deeper chocolate flavor that's great for espresso. Wet processed Ethiopians tend more toward a delicate, floral flavor, occasionally with notes of jasmine or black tea, with a lighter and drier feel on the palate. Yirgacheffe is the best-known wet-processed Ethiopia and has a balanced flavor, often with a bright citrus finish.

Where Ethiopian beans showcase the variety of African coffee, beans from Kenya tend to be much more consistent. Many of the farms in Kenya use the same cultivars, the most prized of which are the SL-28 and SL-34 varieties of the Kent cultivar popularized by British planters. Kenyans are typically wet processed and sun-grown. They often have an acidic savory-sweet flavor that's bold and juicy. There can often be a tomato-like flavor and acidity to Kenyan coffees, or else a puckering tartness similar to the taste of a cranberry or black currant.

Because Kenyans and Ethiopians are the most prominent African coffees, those from other nations are often compared to them. Tanzania, Rwanda, and Zimbabwe produce coffees that are very similar in overall taste profile to Kenyans but with a milder acidity. Coffee from Yemen tastes similar to a dry-processed Ethiopian but with a more fermented flavor that's incredibly complex, with notes of an aged brandy or wine. Coffees from Burundi and Uganda tend to have a lower acidity and heavier body and have natural notes of vanilla or chocolate that tend to come through most clearly with dark roasting.

Southeast Asia and Oceania

Like African coffee, that grown in Southeast Asia and Oceania exhibits a lot of variety from region to region. This is due to variations in both elevation and farming practices; there are a variety of different pruning, cultivation, and processing methods at work in the region. The highest-grown Asian coffees come from Papua New Guinea and the Sulawesi region.

Indonesian coffees are a lot more prominent than most casual coffee drinkers realize. The term "java" became synonymous with coffee because of the popularity of Indonesian blends in the early 20th century. Java is an island in Indonesia, and the coffee grown there tends to work well with medium and dark roast, with low acidity, a heavy, lingering body, and occasional woody notes. This is fairly typical of the Indonesian flavor profile. Many Indonesian coffees have a similar flavor to this, though they can also have a malty, stout-like flavor or a mushroom-like savoriness; the finish is often slightly bitter and lingering like unsweetened dark cocoa. The Sulawesi Toraja is typically processed with the semi-wet style, and has a darker taste than Java, with a spicy fruitiness.

Coffees from the Sumatra region are the main exception to the rule when we talk about the general taste of Indonesian coffees. They tend to be a very divisive coffee, with people either loving their unique taste and texture or hating it. Sumatrans can have a smoky, savory flavor or a fermented, sour fruitiness. The Mandheling varieties tend to be dry processed and have an earthy, dark molasses taste. Coffees of the Gayoland and Aceh varieties are more acidic, with a sweeter, plum or stonefruit taste.

Indonesia isn't the only Pacific nation to produce coffee. Vietnam is one of the few nations known for its robusta, and about 97% of the crops are of this less-heralded species. The coffees from Bali and Papua New Guinea have a similar profile; both tend toward the fruity and do best with lighter roast levels.

JESSICA SIMSS

The Artful Blend

Commercial coffee roasters create blends for one of three reasons: for cost, for consistency, or for complexity. Blending less expensive coffees with pricier options lets the consumer experience those specific notes without having to spend as much to get it. Blends also serve as insurance against the yearly and seasonal variations of certain crops. If one coffee in the blend has a bad year, it can be replaced with something better without having too much impact on the final taste.

As a home enthusiast, the last category is likely to be more your purpose. Making blends at home is usually about combining different notes and taste profiles to create a more satisfying cup more than it is about trying to save a bit on your per-cup costs. This means you'll be shopping for your beans on the basis of their taste profiles, and how well you think they'll work together.

Even if you've studied up on different coffees and their typical notes, figuring out what goes well with what isn't always an easy task. One easy approach is to start off with a base coffee—one that you typically enjoy, or perhaps even your go-to choice. Think about what you would add to the coffee if you could. If it's a chocolatey dark roast, for example, you might want to add something with citrus notes to brighten it up, or maybe something with berry sweetness to mellow out the overall blend.

Find two or three coffees you think would bring these qualities into the blend. Brew up separate pots of all the coffees you plan to include in the blend then mix them together in varying ratios, keeping track of everything you add, until you've found the combination that tastes the most balanced. Using this ratio, whip up a batch of your blend and brew it, to make sure it still gives you the right flavor when you brew it. This method is preferable to blending the beans because it allows you to experiment and taste along the way, fine-tuning the blend without having to brew a new pot each time you make a change.

When you're first experimenting with blends, you'll probably want to limit yourself to two or three coffees maximum in each blend. Even when you are more familiar with flavors and pairings, you shouldn't try to combine more than five. The benefits of blending will start to be canceled out at that point, and you'll more often than not end up with a muddled cup.

You should consider how you typically brew your coffee when you're getting ready to make up a blend. Certain beans and roast levels are better-suited to certain brewing methods. Dark roasts tend to work well as espresso, but may be too bitter when brewed with a drip or pour-over method. Conversely, especially fruity, floral, or acidic light roasts that are bright and complex in the pour-over method can taste sour and thin from an espresso machine. The flavors of coffee tend to intensify as it cools, so if you're making a blend for a cold brew or iced coffee, a milder, medium roast is typically best.

While the popularity of Chemex, pour-over and Aeropress brewing at home has increased in the past few years, most casual coffee drinkers use some version of a drip machine. Drip machines are great brewing methods for mélange blends, a term that refers to combining beans at different roast levels. By using a mélange, you get the deep, roasted flavors of a dark roast balanced by the acid and brighter notes of a light roast, making for a more complex overall cup.

If you're still not sure where to get started, the recipes that follow can perhaps provide some inspiration. All are popular in some variation in the professional coffee community and can be tweaked as needed to suit your own tastes.

Mocha Java

One of the most classic flavor blends in the coffee world is the Mocha-Java blend, which is said to be one of the oldest blends still in use. You'll find that many coffee companies will have their own version of this blend. The exact contents and ratios will vary from place to place, but the overarching idea is the same:

50% Natural-processed Ethiopian, medium or dark roast

50% Sumatra or Java, medium to dark roast

The combination of the sweet, fruity flavor of the Ethiopian beans with the earthier, richer Indonesian coffee results in a cup that's full-bodied with deep chocolatey undertones. If you want to add more brightness and complexity to the flavor, you use two different Ethiopian varieties and a Sumatran or Javan. Start with a ratio of 1 part each then tweak until the flavor is exactly what you're looking for.

Italian Blend

The classic Italian roast is defined by its depth of flavor. It tends to be especially popular with North American drinkers accustomed to the darker roasts served by most large-scale restaurants and coffee shops. The trick with a good Italian blend is to capture those strong roasted flavors without losing the complexity of the overall cup or allowing it to take on a burnt or ashy flavor. A good starting recipe is:

70% Natural-processed Brazil, medium to dark roast

15% Robusta

15% El Salvador or Guatemala, light roast

Putting a bit of robusta into the blend gives it those deep carbon notes that you want in an Italian blend, while the use of a lighter-roasted and milder Central American coffee helps to provide some balance.

Drip Brew Melange

A mélange can be any combination of different roast levels, and if you want to keep things simple, coffees from the same country often complement each other. Using two roast levels of the same bean provides both complexity and balance, with the higher acidity of the lighter roast mellowed by the deeper flavors of the darker roast.

Melanges that integrate coffees from multiple nations can seem more overwhelming. You have to consider not only which regions' beans complement each other but which roast level is right for each component. If you're not sure where to start, try this recipe:

30% Colombian, medium to dark roast

30% Costa Rican, medium to dark roast

40% Kenyan, light roast

Both Colombian and Costa Rican coffees tend to have a caramel sweetness at darker roast levels that will provide a nice compliment to the bright acidity of the Kenyan without overwhelming its sometimes delicate fruity and floral notes.

Espresso Melange

A mélange can also be helpful when you're crafting an espresso blend. Pure light roasts can taste thin or sour, while pure dark roasts can taste ashy or muddled. A mixture of the two can give you the blend of bright citrus notes and deep, chocolatey finish that a good espresso provides. Try starting with a recipe like the following:

60% Mexican, dark roast

40% Natural Ethiopian, light roast

You can adjust the ratio up to 75%/25% if you prefer a darker flavor profile in your espresso. Using a natural Ethiopian has the added benefit of increasing the crema, but if an Ethiopian gives the final cup more fruitiness than you were looking for, try using a dry-processed Central American coffee instead.

Flavored Coffees

Some coffees have flavor notes that are more pronounced than others; some natural processed Kenyans and Ethiopians, for example, can have intense berry flavors, while some coffees from Mexico can taste powerfully of cocoa. Generally, though, the notes in coffee are more subtle. Most blends are designed more with an eye to the overall taste profile of the cup than they are to bringing out a specific flavor. If you want a coffee that actually tastes like vanilla or hazelnut, you'll need to add more than just different kinds of coffee beans into the mix.

You'll find a lot of different flavor options in the coffee aisle of the supermarket. Most of these commercial coffees get their extra flavor from a mixture of chemicals, which is adhered to the beans using a syrup or other binding agent. These residues can be left behind in your grinder and coffee maker, affecting the flavor of your other coffee for weeks afterward. What's more, manufacturers will often use their flavored coffee offerings as a way to get rid of their lower-quality beans, since the taste of this artificial flavoring is so strong it completely obscures all but the most powerful notes in the coffee. By adding your own flavorings, you can make sure you're only using natural ingredients and quality coffee beans. You also get to control the balance of the coffee to the added flavors, allowing the natural notes of the beans to shine through.

Coffee beans are naturally porous, absorbing flavors that are nearby. This can be a bad thing if you're storing your coffee beans in the freezer but is great when you're trying to flavor your beans, as they'll naturally pick up the flavors of anything you seal in with them.

There are a few different ingredients you can use to flavor your coffee, some of which can be utilized in a variety of ways for a different level and type of flavor. While none of these will linger in your grinder and coffee maker nearly as long as artificial flavorings, you may want to clean your equipment between flavors, especially if you're using extracts, nuts, or other ingredients that can leave oils behind.

If you use a burr grinder for your coffee beans, make sure to remove any extra spices, fruits, or nuts you've added to your beans, as they can damage or jam the burrs. You may even want to buy a small blade grinder to use with your flavored mixes. These can usually handle hard-shelled add-ins (and even if they are damaged, are much cheaper to replace) and they're easier to clean when it's time to switch to a new flavor.

Extracts

You'll find two kinds of extracts in the baking aisle: real and imitation. Real extracts are made by soaking mashed up ingredients like vanilla pods or cinnamon sticks in a liquid (usually some kind of alcohol) while imitation extracts are made by combining chemicals together that simulate the flavors. When you're using them to flavor coffee, you want to use real extract; imitation flavors are more likely to degrade over time and can have a bitter aftertaste.

Popular extract options that work well with coffee are vanilla, peppermint, cinnamon, coconut, orange, and maple. Use 3-4 tablespoons of extra for a pound of coffee. You'll probably find it easier to dump the beans into a large mixing bowl, tossing in the flavoring, and then pouring it back in the canister, rather than trying to add the extract right into the container.

Whole spices

Spices like cinnamon, cardamom, clove, and ginger pair well with the taste of coffee and can be used to add a bit of extra flavor to your beans. You'll get the most flavor if you crush the spices before putting them into the blend, especially with hard-shelled options like anise and nutmeg. Add about ¼ cup of crushed, whole spices for each pound of coffee beans and allow the flavors to mingle for 3-4 days before brewing.

Ground spices

Ground spices will have a very similar effect on the flavor to whole spices, but they'll need to be utilized a little differently. Rather than pour them in with the beans, you can mix ground spices in with your coffee after it is ground, just before you pour it into the brew basket. This can make it the perfect option for people who want to use a burr grinder but don't want to have to worry about picking the flavoring agents out of their beans. Add about 1/8 teaspoon of spice for every 2 tablespoons of coffee (about the amount you'll use for one serving).

The flavors listed in the "whole spices" section above are equally good options in their ground forms, but you also have other choices when you go this route. Pre-made mixes like pumpkin pie or apple pie spice complement the taste of coffee well, or you could use ground cocoa to enhance the coffee's chocolatey notes. Chicory is a root that's often ground up and added to coffee in France and French-settled regions like New Orleans. Originally used to stretch coffee supplies during lean times, it has a taste similar to coffee but adds a spiciness that pairs especially well with darker roasts.

Nuts

The oils in the nuts are going to impact the flavor of the coffee beans more than the aromatics. Because of this, you'll get the most extra flavor by crushing the nuts first to release those oils, and then tossing them in with the beans. Add about a tablespoon of crushed nuts for every cup of beans to start, and adjust from there to give you the intensity of flavor you're looking for.

Fruit

Fresh fruit has a lot of moisture, which can contribute to the growth of mold in your coffee beans if they're stored together. This leaves you two options if you want to add fruity flavor to your coffee: dried fruit or citrus rinds. Dried berries, cherries, or apricots can bring out the natural fruitiness of light-roasted coffee, though their flavor may be too subtle to be effective with fuller-bodied blends. Citrus peel, on the other hand, can be a great way to brighten up a darker roast. As with nuts, you should start with about a tablespoon for each cup of beans.

Go Blend!

The range of flavors that can be drawn from a coffee bean is truly staggering. It can give you everything from the bright acidity of citrus to the lingering bitterness of dark chocolate—sometimes in a single cup. Honing your palate and creating artful blends are both skills that you have to learn, and like any skill, they take practice to fully develop. Experiment with as many different kinds of coffee as you can and keep track of which ones you like and which you don't. Even as you hone in on which regions and roast levels tend to be most to your liking, go outside your comfort zone every once in a while; you just might find something that surprises you.

Most coffee shops that sell their beans in bulk will let you buy in any quantity. If you're getting a few different kinds to try out, a quarter pound should be enough to brew a few cups and get an overall sense of the coffee, and you won't run the risk of the beans going stale before you use them. Most coffees are at their peak flavor 7-10 days after roasting, so you don't want to let them sit around for too long.

Home-made coffee blends can also make great gifts, especially if you add flavoring. You can use extracts, spices, nuts, and fruits in combination to create your own recipes and make your blends truly unique. Remember that balance is the key. A more mellow coffee will be a better canvas for a lot of bold added flavors than one that already has a lot of depth and complexity.

JESSICA SIMSS

Coffee is notoriously finicky, both as a plant and as a beverage. Slight changes in the growing conditions or roast times can have a big impact on the taste of the bean, and there will always be variations from batch to batch. Don't get frustrated if your blends don't turn out quite the way you expected, and be creative with your flavor combinations. With enough practice and experimentation, you can blend your way to the perfect cup.

Roasting Coffee

How to Roast Green Coffee Beans like a Pro

Bring out the Beans!

Roasting is an important step in developing the flavors of the coffee bean. When the beans first come out of processing, they'll be soft and green—not at all the hard-shelled brown beans, you're likely accustomed to. These green beans would not grind the way a roasted bean does; even if you did manage to get them ground up, their taste in a brewed cup will be flat, thin, and vegetal, more similar to green tea than normal coffee, and not especially appetizing either way.

More happens in the coffee bean during roasting than just a change in color. The roasting process caramelizes the sugars within the bean and allows the oils trapped within the bean's cells to migrate to the surface, releasing all the coffee's notes and flavors. It also alters the acidity and caffeine content of the beans, both of which are at their highest level in the green form and get gradually lower as the roast darkens. The bean also undergoes structural changes as a result of the roasting process, expanding to about twice their original diameter but also losing 1-3 ounces of weight per pound, translating to a significant reduction in density.

People have been roasting coffee before drinking it since the 15th century. The very first coffee roasting implements were invented in the Ottoman Empire and consisted of thin, perforated pans made of metal or porcelain. These pans were held over a flame or a brazier of hot coals and stirred with a spoon while they roasted. Only a small amount of beans could be roasted at once using these devices; further innovation to expand the capacity didn't come about until the mid-17th century, when the first cylinder roasters were used in Egypt.

You'll hear a lot of different terms applied to different qualities of coffee—all of which are affected by the roasting process in some way. Acidity in coffee is different than a sour taste; it's more a feeling, described as "snappiness" or "brightness" when it's sensed on the edges of the tongue. While some people prefer mellower coffees, some acidity is necessary to prevent the beverage from tasting dull or flat. The body of a coffee is another description of its feel. It refers to the density of the coffee and what sensations it elicits on your tongue. You'll hear it described with words like velvety, creamy, or sharp. Both of these qualities are inherent in the bean to some extent but can be finessed through roasting.

Roasting also affects the aroma, balance, and finish of a coffee. Aroma isn't just about how it smells. Many of the most popular notes in coffee are in fact aromas instead of tastes, including most floral or fruity notes. The finish is the taste and sensation left in your mouth after you swallow; this can include lingering flavor notes or a lingering body. The balance describes how the various other aspects of the coffee relate, and is a good overall indicator of a coffee's quality.

The chapters that follow in this book will go into more depth of how these different characteristics inter-relate and exactly what role roasting plays in developing them. They will also explain the commercial roasting process, and how you can replicate it in the comfort of your own home. Truly anyone can be a home roaster, but even if that's not your plan, understanding the ways in which roasting impacts the flavor of the beans will help you to be a better-informed consumer of the beverage.

Green Coffees

The coffee beans everybody thinks of—brown in color with a hard and sometimes glossy outer surface—get their distinctive attributes through the roasting process. Just like many coffee drinkers would likely not recognize a coffee berry growing on a tree, they'd likely be equally confused by the sight of coffee beans when they come out of processing. While they're more recognizable to the average layperson than coffee cherries, they certainly have a very distinctive set of characteristics.

Coffee beans that have finished processing but are not yet roasted are called green coffee. They're named for their color, which can range from a bright, leafy green to a dull yellowish brown, depending on the type of bean and the processing method used. These beans will also differ from roasted coffee beans in their other sensory qualities. They are soft instead of hard and would be spongy to the bite if you were to eat one. Their smell is vegetal or grassy, more similar to fresh green tea leaves than to what you'd expect from the smell of coffee; if you were to eat an unroasted coffee bean, it would have a similar taste to its aroma, without the rich body or various flavor notes you'd expect to find in the bean.

It is the roasting of the bean that brings out its well-known flavors. The roasting process causes chemical changes within the bean, altering its composition on a molecular level and releasing the oils and other flavor compounds. The extent and nature of these changes will vary depending on how long the bean is roasted; finding the right roast level to bring out the flavors you want from a given bean is part of what makes roasting an art as well as a science.

An unroasted coffee bean contains somewhat higher levels of acids, proteins, sugars, and caffeine than the roasted version. Generally speaking, the longer a bean is roasted, the lower its acidity will be and the less caffeine it will contain per bean, as these compounds are both "roasted out" to some degree. Unroasted beans are also smaller and denser, and the roasted version will be both larger in diameter and lighter in weight than the green bean it started as.

There is no one green coffee bean that is inherently better than the others. While there are some traits you want to look out for that are general hallmarks of quality, most of the attributes of a coffee bean are very personal to your tastes. "Origin flavor" is the term given to the taste characteristics that are inherent within the coffee bean. The origin flavors set the parameters for what is possible in the final cup; how the coffee is roasted will determine which of these characteristics are brought out and which are submerged.

Buying green coffee

You're not likely to find unroasted coffee beans for sale in your local supermarket, or even on the shelf of your local café. Large commercial roasting operations typically source their green bean stock directly from a farm or processing center in its country of origin. Smaller commercial roasters may instead go through a wholesaler that's based in their home nation. In either case, though, these shipments are only available in bulk sacks that contain 50-100 pounds of the same kind of bean—an impractically large quantity for a hobbyist.

For coffee enthusiasts who want to roast their own beans at home, there are two main places to look for unroasted coffee: a local roaster, or an online retailer. Not every independent coffee roaster will be able to sell its green beans to customers. They may purchase their stock to be exactly what they'll need for their upcoming roasting schedule, or may not have a pricing system in place for selling quantities of green beans to customers. They also aren't going to have the same wide variety of options you can find online and may not use the beans you're looking for, especially if you had a specific region or cultivar in mind.

If there is a shop that roasts on-site in your city it's often worth it to at least ask if they'll sell you unroasted beans, especially when you're first starting out. The main advantage of going through an in-person roaster rather than an online vendor is that you can physically examine the green beans before buying them. You can see where the roaster stores them and whether it's appropriate to maintain the bean quality and can feel, smell, or taste the beans themselves to make sure they're fresh and unblemished. The people who work at the roaster will also be an asset. They'll be able to answer questions about what roast levels are right for a given bean or give you tips about your roasting process or equipment. Even if you can't buy your green beans from a local roaster, you may find it valuable to form a relationship with them for this reason.

In most situations, online retailers will be the most convenient way to purchase unroasted coffee beans. They will certainly offer you the most variety, both in terms of cultivar and origin and in terms of quantity. Some online retailers will even offer sampler or variety packs, helpful for beginning roasters who want to experiment with a variety of flavors. While you won't be able to ask questions about the beans, most packages you buy will come with a roast recommendation printed on the label, which is a good starting point when you're experimenting with a new variety. As you may be able to guess, the main disadvantage of an online retailer is that you'll be making your purchase without seeing, smelling, or feeling the beans. You won't know just what you're getting until the beans arrive in your home, and it will be harder to judge the environment in which the green beans have been stored.

Regardless of where you purchase green beans, you'll probably find it to your advantage to buy smaller quantities of a wider variety of bean types and origins, rather than buying several pounds of the same coffee. This will give you a chance to try out a few different flavor profiles and experiment more as you're getting your bearings. It's also probably a good idea to hold off on buying especially rare or expensive beans until you've solidified your technique so you don't have to feel guilty about throwing away failed batches. Prices of green beans will vary greatly depending on the region and cultivar you're purchasing, though as a rule, they'll be significantly cheaper than the same quality and quantity of pre-roasted coffee. In most cases, you can find them for around $5-$10 per pound.

Aged coffee

This is one designation you'll want to look out for when you're shopping for unroasted coffee beans. True aged coffee is stored in its country of origin, often at the same farm or plant where it was processed. It is kept for several months in climate-controlled conditions at a high altitude and turned frequently to discourage bacteria growth. When properly done, the aging process reduces the acidity in the bean, resulting in a mellower, more complex flavor that is highly prized among some enthusiasts. Because it's a more labor- and time-intensive process, however, these aged coffees also carry a higher price tag, even in their unroasted forms.

What the buyer should be wary of are coffees that have been inappropriately labeled as "aged" when they really mean "old." Some unscrupulous sellers will try to get rid of back stock of beans that have been sitting around their warehouse for a few months by labeling them as aged beans. These beans have not received the same care and attention as truly aged coffees and may be stale, flat, or even moldy by the time they reach your door. Unless you've researched the seller and are sure that the beans were handled correctly, it's typically best to avoid any green beans labeled as "aged," especially when you're making your purchase online and can't examine the beans in question.

Storing green coffee

The general rule of thumb for storing green coffee is that if it's comfortable for a person, it's a suitable environment for unroasted beans. By the time they've made it through processing and are ready for shipment and storage, the moisture content in a coffee bean is as low as 10%. Unlike roasted beans (which are extremely porous and act like a sponge, absorbing the moisture, aromas, and flavors they're stored around) green beans are very dense and will not be overly affected by the tastes or smells of things stored nearby, so long as the humidity is kept at a relatively constant, low level.

The ideal environment for a bean is away from direct sunlight in a relatively dry environment that's a comfortable room temperature (in the high 60s or low 70s Fahrenheit). Green coffee should not be stored in the fridge or freezer. This is more an issue of moisture than it is one of temperature. The environment inside a refrigerator is too moist for green coffee beans and could promote bacteria growth; the environment inside a freezer is too dry and could cause the beans to become desiccated and lose flavor.

Green coffee beans maintain their peak flavor up to a year after they finish processing, which gives you a pretty broad window for using them. Make sure to account for how long they spent in storage and shipment before making it to your home when determining the age of your coffee beans, and to use them within one year of the date they left the processing facility (not necessarily a full year after they reached your home).

The kind of container that's best for storing green coffee beans will also be a bit different than those used for roasted beans. Again, green coffee beans tend to be more forgiving than those that have been roasted. In larger roasting operations, coffee beans are typically shipped and stored in burlap bags in large warehouses. At home, you want to use some kind of container that's breathable but secure, keeping contaminants out while letting air in. Don't use airtight containers of plastic, glass, or metal, as these can lead to a build-up of moisture and promote the growth of bacteria or fungus. A paper or cloth bag is ideal, but cardboard boxes and wicker baskets can work just as well provided they're thoroughly closed and secured.

Basic Roasting Processes

Regardless of what kind of roaster you're using and how dark of a roast you're ultimately going for with your coffee, the basic process of roasting beans is the same across the board, though the specifics of timing and temperature will differ method to method. Understanding the different stages of the roast will help you control the ultimate flavor of your cup, and will also help you start to appreciate how and why different levels of roasting bring different tastes to the forefront of the finished beverage.

The ultimate goal of roasting is to achieve the right balance between the original character of the bean and the roast character you bring to it. The ideal balance will depend on the type of bean and the tastes of the drinker, but there are basic guidelines you can follow. Generally speaking, if you prefer darker roasts, what you're looking for are more of the roast characteristics; if you prefer lighter roasts, your tastes are more geared toward the origin character. For most beans, coffee experts would tell you that the "ideal" roast is a light or light-medium because it preserves more of the original flavor of the bean, but this is, again, only a guideline; there is no single right way to roast any given bean.

One of the most important things to keep in mind as you're reviewing all the steps of the roasting process is to use all of your senses as you go through the process. You should never attempt to roast by time and temperature alone. Watch the beans throughout the process to track their color changes, and keep your ears open to listen for the cracks. You can also use your nose to tell how the beans are roasting. The smell of roasting coffee is different than that of brewing coffee, but is equally distinctive; you'll learn what smells indicate your roast is nearly done once you've gone through the process a couple of times. Once the roasting is finished you'll be able to use touch and taste, refining your process for the next time you roast to bring out the character and texture you're looking for.

As was mentioned above, the exact time, temperature, and set-up will vary greatly depending on what method of roasting you're using. The exact details of those processes will be outlined later in the book. Regardless of the method, though, the beans will go through the basic stages outlined below. Not every roast has to go through all of the stages. The roast can be considered complete at any point after the beans have undergone their first crack; continuing to apply heat after this point will darken the roast, so long as the heat application is continuous. Once the beans are removed from the roaster, however, they shouldn't be put back on the heat. The chemical changes that the bean undergoes will not resume once the roast is halted. Returning the beans to heat once they're removed will only scorch the outside of the beans, giving them an ashy, burnt taste.

Yellowing

The first few minutes of the roasting process are referred to as yellowing because of the color changes that take place in the beans. It is an endothermic stage of the roast, meaning the beans are actively absorbing the heat applied to them by the roaster, using this to start the chemical processes that will take place inside the beans. If you're watching the beans at this point you'll see them gradually lose their greenish tint and instead turn a pale brown or yellow color.

The moisture enclosed within the bean will begin to steam toward the end of this process—not enough steam yet to alter the structure of the bean, but enough to put off a definite aroma. This will start off as a grassy smell that gradually shifts to an aroma more like toast or popping popcorn as it gets toward the end of this stage.

First crack

Where the yellowing is named for what you'll see, the first crack gets its name from what you'll hear. The first crack is the point in the roast where the gasses and steam within the bean build up so much pressure they force their way through, breaking the physical structure of the bean along the seam down its center. It is the first pyrolytic reaction in coffee roasting, which is a term that generally refers to a reaction within a substance to the application of heat. If you're tracking the time and temperature of the roast, the first crack will happen once the beans reach around 390° F, which will be anywhere from 3 to 15 minutes into the roast, depending on your method, and usually lasts from 1 to 3 minutes.

The sound of the first crack is very distinctive. It sounds similar to snapping wooden toothpicks, or a slightly sharper version of the sound of popcorn popping. Like popcorn, the first crack tends to start slowly, building to a louder and more forceful, continuous crackling sound before tapering off and slowing toward the end. This is the stage at which the most water weight is lost within the bean, and also the point at which the diameter increases the most, with most of the expansion happening because of structural cracks in the bean caused by escaping moisture. Your other senses will be useful during the first crack, as well. The aroma will shift, picking up more of a burnt sugar aroma, with the steam beginning to darken into smoke. By the end of the first crack, the beans should be a light brown color, with slight mottling and a bumpy, matte surface.

The pace of the roast accelerates following the first crack, so it is important to maintain a close watch over the beans once they've completed this stage. The fissures made by the escaping steam allow more heat to enter the core, causing the oils trapped there to migrate toward the surface. This is also the point that the sugars within the beans begin to caramelize, bringing out the sweet and fruity aspects of the original characteristics.

Caramelization

Once the first crack is finished, the roast can be considered complete at any point. They'll reach the level of a light or City roast between 30 and 90 seconds after the end of the first crack; leaving the beans in the roaster after this point simply continues the work of caramelization, darkening the roast and shifting the balance between origin and roasting characteristics. The interior temperature of the bean at this point will be between 415°F and 445°F and will quickly go through the City + and Full City stages of the roast.

If you're looking for a specific roast level between the first and second cracks, your eyes and nose will be the best indicators. Visually, you'll see the beans continue to expand in size, with the surface becoming darker and smoother as the roast progresses. You'll start to see cracks forming at the tips of the beans, as well, as trapped moisture and carbon dioxide continue to force their way to the outside air. The smell will shift, as well, with more of a heavy malty character that may have herbal, sweet, or floral notes imbued with the bean's original characteristics. This will continue to get darker and heavier, changing to a bittersweet chocolate or burnt sugar, caramel note as it gets closer to the end of the stage.

Second crack

The second pyrolytic reaction during the roasting process is known as the second crack. Generally speaking, this marks the point at which the roast character will begin to assert itself over the origin character. It is a deeper fracturing of the structure than the first crack, actually affecting the cellular matrix of the bean. This lets the oils within the cells finally migrate to the bean's exterior, giving the beans the oily, shiny surface common in darker roasts.

The second crack has a different sound than the first crack. It is shallower but faster and more volatile, often described as sounding like the snap, crackle, and pop of rice cereal in milk, or alternatively like an electrical sparking sound. In some cases, the crack is so volatile it sends small shards of the beans flying away like shrapnel. Even though it is a more constant sound than the first crack, the sound of the second crack should never blur into one continuous noise. If you can't differentiate between the different sounds in the second crack, the heat of the roast was likely too high, and your coffee may be burnt; try using lower heat during your next roast.

The second crack tends to start around 440°F and can continue through the point where the beans are around 470°F. Changes within the bean happen very quickly during these stages; a matter of mere seconds can separate a Vienna Roast from an Italian Roast, from a coffee that is officially over-roasted. You'll have to pay especially close attention to the sensory cues the beans are giving you once you reach the second crack. The beans will darken to a chocolatey brown with large cracks at the tips and visible oil on the surface, while the smell will become very bitter and rich, like dark chocolate. The smoke coming out of the beans will be more pungent and thicker at this stage as the sugars continue to caramelize and the bean structure breaks down more and more.

Roasted too far

Once the beans get above a temperature of about 470°F, they'll be too dark for even Italian-roast lovers to tolerate. The sugars in the beans will have burned off completely and none of the bean's origin characteristics will remain. At this point, it doesn't matter where the beans come from or what their taste potential was; all beans will taste the same, with an ashy, bitter, thin taste that some coffee experts have described as "charcoal water"—not an especially appetizing brew.

Cooling

The heat trapped within the beans means they will continue to develop for a little while after you remove them from the heat. The longer you roasted the beans, the more residual heat will be trapped within them even after the flame is removed. Because of this, you always want to remove the beans from the roaster when they're slightly lighter than your ideal level. Finding this sweet spot is a matter of practice, and is as much a matter of feel and instinct as it is a result of the sensory cues the beans are giving you.

Keeping the beans in motion and allowing for continuous airflow over their surfaces is important to maintain the consistency of the roast level. Again, the longer and darker the beans were roasted, the more important it is to ensure even airflow during the cooling stage. The beans will also continue to release carbon dioxide and pent-up moisture for several hours after the roasting has finished, and will need to be stored in such a way that allows them to breathe for 12-24 hours post-roasting.

Roast Levels

Many commercial roasters will give their own names to their coffees, which describe both the variety and the roast level of the beans. This lack of industry standard can make it a bit difficult to determine the exact roast level of your favorite coffee for home replication. If the coffee is from a local roaster, they may be willing to give you the inside scoop on their temperature, timing, and roast level for certain beans. Otherwise, you can use sensory information, like the color and aroma of the beans, to get you close to the right level, but finding an exact match will likely take a lot of trial and error.

Roast levels are often given geographical names just like the growing regions of the coffees are. The difference is that the names of roast levels are derived from the popularity of these roasting styles in various areas of the world, not a description of where the beans are grown. Understanding where coffees grow in the world will help you to tell whether a place name describes the bean or the roast. Anything from Europe will be a roast descriptor by default because coffee doesn't grow in those areas. The European preference is for dark roasts, and all of the European roast labels describe coffees that have been allowed to undergo their second crack. American tastes tend to run lighter, with those on the East Coast generally preferring light and medium roasts and those on the West Coast leaning toward medium or medium-dark varieties.

If a coffee is described as "underdeveloped," this means its roasting process was halted before the beans went through the necessary chemical reactions to bring out the flavor and sweetness of the bean—in other words, that the beans never made it to their first crack. On the other side of things, an "over-developed" bean is one that spent too long in the roasting chamber between the first and second cracks. This results in a cup of coffee that has flat, muted flavors, almost no acidity, and a thin body.

There are four broad categories of roasting level, defined by the color of the bean when it's finished: light, medium, medium-dark, and dark. There are no hard and fast boundaries between these categories, though there some general characteristics shared by coffees at the same roast level; these are described in the sections that follow below.

Light roasts

A light roast is typically the best roast level for mild coffees, and also tends to be preferred for those coffees with delicate floral notes or other subtle flavors, allowing these tastes to shine through without obstruction. Because it allows the most original characteristics of the bean to be tasted, it is also the preferred roast level for highly-prized or expensive coffees, such as Geishas or Blue Mountain cultivars.

Light roasts retain almost all of the caffeine contained inside the bean. They'll also tend to have a very pronounced acidity, which at its best could be described as bright, with assertive fruity or sweet flavors, and at its worst would be described using words like strident or sour, with flavor notes that are grassy, green, or vegetal. The roast character will be subtle, with more of a toasted grain flavor than the bold, dark nutty and chocolate notes associated with deeper roast levels. In appearance, light-roasted beans will have a pale brown color, sometimes mottled with darker brown spots. They tend to be quite dense with no visible cracking or oil and a somewhat bumpy, uneven surface.

You'll see light roasts described by an array of other terms. The most common are City, Light City or Half City; you may also see it called a New England Roast because of the popularity of lighter roasts along the eastern seaboard of the United States. In some circles, a light roast is known as a Cinnamon Roast because of the color of the surface, though this term can also be used to refer to an even paler version of the bean that is removed from roasting just at the end of the first crack.

Medium roasts

A medium roast level is the most popular in North America, and for many cultivars and growing regions, it is considered to be the ideal roast level for balancing origin and roast characteristics in the final cup. Compared to light roasts, these coffees will have a fuller body, a lower acidity, and slightly less caffeine. The toasted grain roasting flavor of light roasts will be gone, replaced by a smoother, deeper roast profile that has a more pronounced aroma. If the bean had a sour taste at a light roast level, roasting to a medium level should reduce this without eliminating the fruity or sweet notes you're hoping to bring out of the bean.

A medium roast is sometimes also called an American Roast because of its popularity in the United States. You may also see it called a Full City Roast, City + Roast, Breakfast Roast, or Regular Roast. The surface will still lack any visible oil, though it will be a more consistent and slightly darker hue of brown than light-roasted beans, and you may see a small amount of cracking at the ends of the seam on the flat part of the coffee bean.

Medium-dark roasts

The medium-dark roast is usually obtained by stopping the roast just before the second crack, or in its very first stages. This roast will generally have the most body of any roast level, even compared to darker roasts, with less acidity and caffeine than the same bean at a lighter roast. Depending on how long into the second crack the roast is halted, you may see a small amount of oily sheen on the surface of the bean, which will otherwise be a uniform deep brown, with visible cracking around the ends of the bean and an otherwise smooth surface.

Medium-dark roasts will have a rich flavor with a slightly bitter aftertaste. The roast characteristics will be slightly more assertive than the origin characteristics at this roast level, though you should still be able to taste fruity, nutty, or chocolate notes. This gives medium-dark roasts a complexity that many people prize, with a bittersweet finish. In fact, for coffees with generally darker origin characteristics, many people consider them to be the most balanced at a medium-dark roast instead of a straight medium, though more delicate coffees are likely to have their origin characteristics overwhelmed by the depth of flavor.

You may also see this called a Full City or an After Dinner Roast. Some beans labeled as Vienna Roasts will also be medium-dark, though that's a designation you may see applied to full dark roasts, as well. A lot of coffee shops consider medium-dark roasts to be ideal for espresso, giving the flavor a depth that's not overwhelming and works especially well with quick extraction methods.

Dark roasts

A dark roast is the darkest roast level you can achieve while still maintaining the quality and flavor of the beverage. It is loosely defined as any bean that is allowed to roast through the second crack. Dark roasts, in general, will have a pronounced bitterness, often with a smoky or burnt aftertaste, and the original character will be thoroughly submerged by the roast character. They will also have the lowest caffeine and acidity levels, with a less pronounced body than medium-dark roasts. In terms of the appearance, dark roasts will have a shiny, smooth surface that can range in color from dark brown to nearly black. They will be the largest and least dense beans, as well, with visible cracks at both ends of the bean and a relatively brittle interior structure.

You're likely to find the most name variations for dark roasts, many of which will have a different meaning depending on the roaster, making it the most confusing roast level to interpret accurately. All of the European place names are dark roasts; from lightest to darkest, these are Vienna, Spanish, French, and Italian. You may also see dark roasts called Continental Roasts generally, referring to some variant of a European roast. Other common names for dark roasts are New Orleans Roast and high Roast. The lighter of the dark roasts—including Vienna and Continental—come from the very start of the second crack and are commonly used for espresso. By the time the roast reaches the level of an Italian, the sugars are burned away almost completely, giving the coffee a thin, bitter aroma and taste.

Choosing Your Roast

As has been mentioned before, there is no hard and fast rule about what roast level is right for a specific coffee. The main advantage of roasting your own beans at home is being able to make your coffee exactly the way you like to drink it, whether or not that's the way your local coffee shop would treat it. Having said that, there are roast levels for certain coffees that are generally believed to bring out the best the bean has to offer. Especially when you're first experimenting with roasting, these recommendations can make excellent starting points.

Even perfect roasting can't imbue notes or complexity into a bean that weren't there to begin with. It is fairly common practice in commercial coffee roasting to use less flavorful beans for darker roasts in the hopes that the roast character can add some interest to an otherwise bland or flat cup, but the best way to achieve high-caliber roasts is to use high-caliber beans. Because green beans will cost less per pound than they would pre-roasted, home roasting provides an excellent opportunity to drink top tier coffees without having to pay top tier prices—and ultimately meaning you have no excuse not to use the best beans available to you.

Of course, if you're a relative newcomer to the coffee world, identifying which beans are the best can be tricky. While some coffee-producing nations have their own side or quality grading systems, there is no international standard to rank the quality of coffee. Beans that have won Cup of Excellence awards or other competitions are obvious good choices, but since taste is such a subjective quality, even these coffees aren't necessarily guaranteed to provide you with your ideal coffee. Gaining a basic understanding of what contributes to the flavor notes of different beans is the best way to figure out which regions, climates, and processing methods are the right ones for your palate; the book on harvesting coffee earlier in this series is an excellent resource if you're hoping to learn this kind of information.

The sections that follow in this chapter will focus more on matching beans to the right roast level than on the particular notes or flavors. While there are a plethora of factors that determine the ultimate flavor of a coffee bean, the three that are most important, in order, are the bean's origin, the cultivar or variety, and the processing method. Washed-processed beans have a cleaner profile that's generally brighter and more vibrant, leading to them often being treated as light and medium roasts. Natural or dry-processed beans are typically more complex, with more depth, body, and often an assertive fruitiness or earthiness. These flavors can be too assertive when they're roasted light, and they typically favor a medium to a medium-dark. Combine this information with the general guidelines for the different coffee growing regions outlined below to find the perfect roast for your beans.

Africa

The birthplace of coffee, Africa still is the growing region where you'll find the most variety in terms of farming methods, processing methods, and flavor profiles. Kenya and Ethiopia are the best-known coffee growing countries in Africa, but you'll also find beans grown in other nations, including Tanzania, Uganda, Burundi, and Rwanda, just to name a few. Coffees grown in the Middle East are also generally considered in the same category as African coffees because they share many of the same characteristics.

Regardless of the country, the majority of coffees from Africa are grown on small farms using fairly traditional methods. There is limited application of commercial pesticides and fertilizers, with most trees grown in intermixed plots that closely simulate the plant's growing environment in the wild. In fact, the nations of northern and central Africa are the only ones that regularly harvest the cherries from wild coffee trees. Because so many of their coffees are grown in small batches, you also may have some difficulty finding beans from the same farm or region consistently throughout the year, especially if you have your heart set on a particular cultivar. This makes it especially important to be able to identify just what it is about the region (elevation, climate, etc.) that gives you the flavors that you're looking for. Both washed and natural processing methods are employed throughout the continent, as well, further complicating decisions about the right level of roast.

African coffees, in general, tend to do well with a light to medium roast, which allows the naturally sweet and fruity notes to shine through. This is especially true of Ethiopian coffees, which already tend to have a rather thick, syrupy body and can be overly full if roasted to a medium-dark level. Coffees from Kenya are the general exception to this rule. Because they're very bold with high acidity, some people like to use a medium-dark roast for Kenyan beans. The origin characteristics are assertive enough to stand up to darker roast flavors, and the extra time in roasting mellows out the brightness inherent in the bean.

South America

Some of the world's largest coffee producers are in South America. Although the continent's growing region is comparable in size to that in Africa, there is generally less variation both in terms of climate and in farming practices. Coffees from a specific country will generally hold the same basic characteristics and will do well with the same roast levels with some exceptions.

The countries which grow the most coffee in South America are Colombia and Brazil. You can consider Colombia to be the standard South American coffee—and in fact is the definition of "good coffee" so far as most Americans are concerned, being the kind of coffee that is most familiar to North American palates. The elevation at which the coffee is grown will determine which is the best roast level for a given bean. The higher-grown the coffee, the lighter you'll want to roast it. Medium- or low-grown Colombians will typically taste best when roasted to an American Roast level, which is a solid medium to medium-dark. This same wisdom will hold true of coffees from Peru, Venezuela, or other South American nations.

Brazil is the exception to this rule. There is a much wider variation in climates in Brazil than in the other South American nations. As a result, much of the coffee from this country is lower-grown, giving it the distinction of being the only South American nation where Robusta is grown in nearly the same quantities as Arabica. Even the Arabica beans from Brazil tend to be larger in size and milder in flavor, and tend to have a relatively heavy mouthfeel with rich, chocolate notes. This makes them ideal for medium-dark or dark roasts, especially if you plan to use them in an espresso blend, which the Robustas of Brazil are especially popular for. If you have a higher-grown coffee from Brazil, or beans from the Bahia region, a medium roast will give you the best balance and complement the mild, low-acidity of the bean.

Central America and Islands

There are some similarities between the coffees of Central and South America; both regions tend to produce generally bright coffees with a pronounced sweetness and fruity or citrus undertones. The main difference between these regions is the average elevation. Coffees from Central America tend to be higher-grown, which produces denser beans with more flavor complexity.

Coffees from Costa Rica are the most consistent of all the beans from this region. Not only do most of the country's farms use the same basic practices and array of cultivars, many of these farms process their beans at the same centralized facilities, and are almost invariably washed. Other Central American nations like Guatemala, Honduras, Nicaragua, Panama, and Belize also produce very high-quality coffee, generally mild and often with delicate, floral notes. These nations have not been as well-known to American coffee drinkers, in large part because political upheaval and serious hurricanes have limited their crop production since the 1990s. Many of these beans are starting to make a comeback on today's artesian coffee market, however, and have in many cases made quite a splash. The Geisha cultivar from Panama was for a time the most expensive coffee on the market, and other Central American cultivars have won high honors in international cupping competitions.

Because of their delicacy and exceptional flavor, Central American coffees are generally better-suited to lighter roasts. They do tend to be brighter coffees with a relatively high acidity; to balance this out, some people prefer a medium to a light roast for coffees from this region. Anything darker than a medium roast will obscure the complex origin characteristics of the bean and is not recommended.

Though they are geographically disparate areas—and the growing conditions are often very different—coffees from islands in both the Caribbean and the Pacific can be considered in the same category as Central American coffees when it comes to determining the roast level. This includes famously high-grown varieties like the Jamaica Blue Mountain, which is consistently one of the priciest and rarest coffees in the world but also includes lower-grown coffees like Hawaiian Kona or Maui, where the relatively new volcanic soil gives the beans a mild floral taste and sweet aroma that are best-suited to light roasts.

Central and Southeast Asia

There was a time that the island of Java produced more beans by volume than anywhere else in the world, so dominating the market that the term "Java" became a synonym for coffee. Though this is no longer the case, nations like Indonesia, India, and Vietnam are responsible for a larger percentage of the world's production than many people likely realize—and also produce some of the most unique and divisive coffees available on the global scale.

When it comes to the Indonesian islands of Sumatra, Java, and Sulawesi, there are two broad categories: those grown on large estates, often government-owned and operated, and those grown on small family holdings. Both will have a dark, earthy quality with notes of unsweetened cocoa, but the Indonesian Estate coffees tend to be much more consistent, especially in the processing stage; they do well at medium roast levels, but will also tolerate darker roasts well without losing their distinctive qualities. Beans from smaller holdings in Indonesia are often allowed to ferment more before drying—either intentionally or due to inconsistencies in the processing methods—which can give the finished bean a sour or smoky quality. This tends to make them better suited to a medium-dark or even a dark roast, which can mask or balance out these notes in the coffee.

You'll be less likely to see coffee from India or Vietnam in the commercial market, but they are nonetheless worth mentioning. Coffees from India vary widely in quality; the majority that make it to export are grown in relatively humid areas with a moderate to high elevation and tend to be roasted either medium or medium-dark. Vietnam's coffee production is almost exclusively Robusta; it is perhaps because of this that the few Arabica varieties grown in the country are almost invariably roasted dark.

Commercial Roasting

While only the most dedicated coffee connoisseurs would even consider roasting their own beans today, home-roasting was the norm for much of the history of the plant's cultivation. The first patents for commercial roasters weren't secured until the mid-nineteenth century, and even then the idea was generally derided by the majority of coffee growers. After all, it seemed like a lot of effort when it was such an easy and popular thing for consumers to do on their own at home.

It wasn't until the 1870s that commercial roasting technology progressed to the point that the economy of scale made it worthwhile for wide-scale implementation by commercial vendors. These benefits were expanded in 1903 when the invention of the first electric roasters eliminated the problem of fuel vapor and smoke giving the roasted coffee an off taste. As commercial coffee roasting equipment grew more sophisticated, it also allowed for a finer control of the roast level and temperature, as well as the expansion of batch sizes, all of which contributed to a gradual shift in the United States from nearly exclusive home roasting in the early 1800s to nearly exclusive commercial roasting by the 1930s.

Today's commercial coffee roasting operations come in a wide array of styles. The largest coffee companies, like Starbucks or Folgers, roast their beans in massive batches in centralized facilities, typically using fully-automated equipment that can roast beans consistently to the same level even without direct human supervision. Smaller commercial roasters will often employ designated roast masters who watch over the beans throughout the process, listening for the crack and using their other senses to gauge the roast level in much the same way as a hobbyist would roasting at home; in fact, aside from the level of expertise involved, the main difference between these smaller commercial roasters and a home operation are the size and frequency of batches produced. A commercial roaster can prepare batches of up to 30 kilograms at one time, and some can produce as much as a ton of beans per day.

Just like with home roasting operations, the exact process used for commercial roasting will differ depending on the size and set-up of the company. They may operate in batches or run their machines on a continuous cycle, for example, and can use a variety of different roasting equipment, from the most sophisticated and modern automated models to home-grown drum roasters that essentially consist of a steel garbage can rotating over a flame. There are certain constants in the equipment and process, however, the general details of which are outlined in the sections that follow.

Commercial roasting equipment

There are a variety of different options on the market when it comes to commercial roasting equipment, including packed bed, tangential, and centrifugal models that are very different from the kind of roasting most people are familiar with. In general, however, two kinds of roasters are the most prevalent in the commercial roasting market: fluid bed roasters and drum roasters.

Drum roasters were the commercial standard for many years, and use a relatively simple principle to accomplish large-batch, efficient roasting. Generally speaking, these consist of a rotating metal drum that contains the beans, turning them gradually over some kind of flame or heat source maintained underneath the drum to accomplish the roasting. You may also find direct-fired roasters that use the drum concept, in which the flame comes into direct contact with the beans themselves. These were more common in the past than they are today, though you may still find a few in operation here or there. The majority of drum roasters today use an indirect heat source, which can be fueled electronically, by using natural gas or liquefied petroleum, or the old-fashioned way by burning wood; some highly advanced drum roasters will use what's known as an industrial ribbon burner, which keeps the temperature even across the entire length of the flame. The motion of the drum makes sure that the beans don't stay in one place for too long, preventing the surface of the beans from scorching and promoting a more even roast across the batch. Drum roasters typically have a larger potential capacity than other commercial roasting equipment while still allowing for fine-tuning of the temperature and roast level, making them especially popular for use with complex roasts and blends.

Fluid bed roasters, on the other hand, use the direct application of heated air to the beans to both circulate and roast them simultaneously. In this method, the hot air is pushed through a metal screen with enough force that it lifts and tumbles the beans, circulating them within the roasting chamber; this layer of forced air is referred to as a fluidized bed, which is what gives this particular roasting method its name. A fluid bed roasting method will produce a brighter roast with less chance of scorching or over-roasting but also does not permit the same level of control of the temperature as a drum roaster.

Both drum and fluid bed roasters come in various levels of automation. Those that are primarily human-controlled will typically have a small window on the front of the machine through which the roast master can track the color changes in the beans to ensure they're being roasted to the right level without interrupting the roasting process or opening the drum, reducing the chance of variations in the roast temperature. Visual and olfactory indicators can be especially important for roasting on a large scale, as many of these industrial-sized roasters can be quite loud, making it difficult for the roast master to hear the first and second cracks. Fully-automated roasters, on the other hand, can be set to release the beans into a cooling chamber either after a designated length of time or when the bean temperature reaches a certain level.

Commercial roasting process

When commercial roasters purchase their green beans, they'll often buy six months' to a year's supply of beans at one time. These beans come in large burlap sacks that weigh around 100-130 pounds each, depending on the density of the beans themselves. These sacks of beans are stored in large temperature-controlled warehouses until they're ready to be used; depending on the size of the operation, these warehouses may be owned by the roasting company itself or by the distributor, who then sends them to the roaster on a regular schedule when they're ready to be used.

The main difference between various roasting processes is largely dependent on the degree of automation. The bags of green beans are emptied into a hopper when they're about to be used, a process which may be done by hand or by machines. From there, the beans are screened to remove any debris like stems, leaves, or husks that have stayed attached to the beans through processing before being conveyed to the roaster itself. Again, this can be done with an automated conveyor or by using human-powered carts.

Once the beans have been roasted to the correct level, they're emptied into cooling machines. In most commercial operations, the cooling is accomplished mechanically in specialized equipment that keeps the beans in constant motion while air is allowed to flow through the beans via a perforated metal grate underneath the beans. Cooling has to be carefully regulated, especially when roasters are preparing large batches of ten or more pounds. If the beans cool too fast, they'll get stale too quickly, losing their peak flavor before they have a chance to be brewed. If they cool too slowly, the residual heat in the beans will cause them to be over-roasted; too many of the sugars in the beans will be caramelized, resulting in a cup that's flat or acrid.

Once they're cooled, the roasted beans are ready to be bagged for distribution. If they're going out to a café for in-house use, they'll be divided into large, breathable bags that allow the residual carbon dioxide to escape; if they're being vacuum-sealed for retail sale, they'll be allowed to rest for 12-24 hours prior, until these gasses have had a chance to dissipate. In either case, the roasted beans will often go through a second sorting that screens out anything heavier than a coffee bean. This prevents small objects like stones or screws from making their way into the final beans—items that can badly damage a grinder if they make it through the process undetected.

Home Roasting

As you learned in the last chapter, home roasting was the standard until the mid-nineteenth century, and commercial roasting wasn't the standard until almost a hundred years later. For the modern consumer, of course, coffee beans most often arrive in their pre-roasted form—sometimes even pre-ground, if you tend to buy your coffee from the supermarket. You can find specialized home roasting equipment for sale in coffee specialty shops, and this equipment can make the process as technical and exacting as you want to make it. It doesn't take any kind of specialized equipment to roast your own beans at home, though; people roasted coffee at home for centuries, even before the advent of modern kitchen appliances and technology. With a bit of knowledge—and some practice—you can easily roast beans exactly to the level you like right in the comfort of your own kitchen.

The basic principles behind roasting coffee are the same as those for popping corn; in fact, some of the best home coffee roasters are re-purposed air popcorn poppers. Because coffee beans contain a certain amount of oil already, you won't need to add any oil when you roast them (and you also won't be able to roast them in the microwave). The main practical difference with roasting coffee at home from a planning perspective is that the process will generate a significant amount of smoke. The darker you like your coffee roasted, the more smoke will be produced. This means you'll want to do your roasting in a well-ventilated area. If this isn't possible in your kitchen, you'll probably want to set up a camp stove or other heat source outside.

Coffee will also release chaff when it roasts. Chaff is the papery outer covering of the bean. It's tasteless and won't cause a problem if it stays mixed in with the roasted beans, but it can make a mess as it flies off during roasting—something else to keep in mind if you're doing it in your kitchen. Some chaff is also likely to accumulate inside your roaster and will need to be cleaned out between batches; if it isn't, it runs the risk of catching fire when the temperature inside the roaster goes up.

The typical home roasting takes around 10-16 minutes, depending on the size of the batch and the method you're using. Though it's a smaller operation than commercial roasting, it is nonetheless an acquired skill and one that's best honed through practice and experience. The general temperature timelines in chapter 3 and the timings listed here in the various home roasting methods are good guidelines to follow, but to roast successfully, you should focus more on the sight, sound, and smell of the beans than on the clock or thermometer.

Aside from the roasting method itself, there are a few other supplies you'll likely want to have around before you start the process. Though timing and temperature shouldn't be your main deciding factors in telling when a roast is done, it's still important information to have. You'll want to have a thermometer that can read at least 500°F and can be attached to the inside of your roasting device. Don't use glass thermometers, as these run the risk of breaking; infrared thermometers work well if you have an unobstructed view of the roaster's interior. When it comes to the timer, anything that can be operated hands-free and tracks minutes and seconds will work, whether that's a standard kitchen timer or the stopwatch on your phone. Tracking how much coffee you put into the roaster in each batch will also help you track and replicate your successful roasts. A kitchen scale that measures in both grams and ounces is ideal.

Finally, you'll need some tools to help you with the cooling process. The beans will be extremely hot when you remove them from the roaster; keep some hot pads or oven mitts close at hand so you can handle them without injuring yourself. A large metal colander works best for cooling the beans because it allows for airflow from both underneath and above. If you can't find one of these, a large metal bowl will do the trick, though you'll need to stir the roasted beans more aggressively (and for longer) to make sure the beans cool evenly. A long-handled metal or wooden spoon is the best utensil for agitating the cooling beans.

Which roasting method you choose will depend on a variety of factors. Your budget is a big one. A dedicated home roasting appliance will be the most expensive option, costing between $50 and $500 depending on the brand and features; on the other side of the spectrum, many DIY options are functionally free, since you'll use equipment you already have in your home. The lower-tech your roaster, the more you'll need to focus on technique to achieve even, consistent roasts. If you want any automation in the process, a dedicated appliance will be a necessity. You should also consider how much coffee you drink, how large you want to make the batches, and what level of precision you want to achieve in your roasting. The sections that follow in this chapter will outline some of the most popular roasting methods, along with their pros, cons, and best uses.

Roasting log

Tracking what worked and what didn't in your previous attempts at roasting is the best way to learn and solidify your techniques, and the best way to do this is by keeping a detailed log of all your roasts. You can designate a notebook for this task or use a spreadsheet on your computer. Use this to make note of all the details of the process, from the type of beans that you use to how you brew the finished beans (and how they taste when you do).

There are a few key details you should make note of in your log. First, write down the date, the time, and what the weather is like when you start the roast; factors like humidity and air temperature will affect how the beans behave, especially if you're roasting outside. Note any details you have about the beans themselves, at the very least their country of origin, cultivar or variety, and processing method. Also, write down how much coffee you're roasting by weight and the method of roasting.

During the roasting process, you want to record how much heat is applied, along with the timing and temperature in the roasting chamber at key milestones like the first and second crack. You should also record any notable sensory details, like shifts in the aroma and appearance of the beans. Finally, note the time and temperature when you remove the beans from the roaster, as well as the approximate length of the cooling process and the appearance and aroma of the finished product.

You don't have to be a coffee professional to take accurate tasting notes. Simply write down your impressions of the coffee once you get a chance to drink it. Include things like how it smells during grinding and brewing, how it feels in your mouth, and any flavor notes you can identify. You should also jot down anything that you want to improve so you can tweak the process on your next pass.

Roasting appliances

The advantage of buying an appliance designed for roasting coffee is that it will give you a host of features that make roasting quicker, easier, and cleaner. Some of them, like the Nesco Home Coffee Roaster, have smoke-reducing technology, which is very helpful if you want to roast indoors without setting off your fire alarm. Many also have automated controls for setting the time, temperature, and air flow, as well as a catch for the chaff and a set-up that allows you to easily watch the beans without releasing heat.

You can find both drum roasters and fluid bed roasters that are small enough for use in your home. They'll use the same basic technology as commercial versions but sized to roast batches of anywhere from 4 ounces to 2 pounds, depending on the model. They're also not built to handle the same amount of use as a commercial roaster, and in most cases shouldn't be used more than once per day or you'll risk burning them out. With regular use, most will last around two years, and longer if you only use the machine occasionally.

The fluid bed coffee roasters you'll find in the store are a variant of the air poppers mentioned below, but with tweaks that make them better suited for coffee. This usually involves a metal basket that can better handle higher temperatures, an expanded capacity, and easier access to the roasting chamber. Most roasts will take around 8-12 minutes in these machines. The Nesco mentioned above is a good example of a fluid bed roaster, but other popular brands include Fresh Roast, Kaldi, and Gene Café.

Home drum roasters tend to be a bit cheaper than fluid bed models and are also typically built to handle larger batches. If used correctly, they can give you a more even roast than most air roasters, but they also tend to need more practice and attention and will produce more smoke. It takes a bit longer to roast with these machines, around 14-20 minutes on average. Gene Café also sells drum roasters; other popular brands include Behmor and HotTop.

Air poppers

Electric hot air popcorn poppers are essentially less expensive versions of a fluid air bed roaster. You may be able to find one of these used in a second-hand store; they're relatively durable, and even fairly old models should still work for your purposes provided they have a high enough voltage. You can also buy them new for around $20-$50 from kitchen supply and department stores. Good brands to look out for are Toastess, West Bend, Nostalgia, Toastmaster, and Kitchen Gourmet.

Short of buying a designated roaster, this is the most recommended method for roasting at home. It's the best way to get an even roast at any level, from light to dark. Most air poppers have a see-through top or a butter cup you can remove to give you a clear line of sight into the roasting chamber, letting you keep an eye on the progress of your roast. It will produce a decent amount of both smoke and chaff. Because it's electrically powered, though, you can easily use it in a garage, yard, or other outdoor area. If you do want to use it inside, make sure the room is well-ventilated and put a large bowl under the spout of the machine to catch any escaping chaff.

When you're using an air popper, you want to turn it on first before you start pouring the green beans into the chamber. This will start the air flowing through the chamber, making the beans start to spin even as you're adding them. Add the beans slowly, checking periodically to make sure they're still moving smoothly. If the movement of the beans in the chamber starts to look slow or labored, you should stop adding beans; overcrowding the roasting chamber will lead to an inconsistent roast. Depending on the model, most air poppers will be able to handle batches of around 2/3-3/4 cup.

Once the beans are in, put the plastic hood on the machine and wait nearby. In around 3-5 minutes you should hear the first crack. If you want to make a dark roast, it should only take a couple minutes more to get it there, making air popper roasting one of the fastest methods. Remove the beans from the roaster when they're still a shade lighter than the roast level that you're looking for; they'll continue to roast a bit as they're cooling. If possible, dump the beans out of the roast chamber before you turn the machine off. This will prevent the beans from settling against the very hot metal of the chamber, which could cause them to scorch.

If you find your beans are burning or roasting too quickly, the machine might be running at too high a temperature. Try using an extension cord rather than plugging the popper right into the wall; this will slightly reduce the voltage running to the popper, making it run a bit cooler. If it's roasting too slowly, you may be trying to roast too small a batch for the size of the chamber. The air temperature won't rise unless it meets some resistance from the beans. Try using a larger batch next time, as well as keeping the roaster away from any drafts or other sources of cool air.

Stovetop poppers

A stovetop popper will give you the most similar roast profile to a commercial drum roaster. These devices can technically be used to roast to any level, although lighter roasts will be more difficult to achieve consistently. Stovetop poppers can roast a slightly higher volume of coffee than air poppers, up to a pound at a time depending on the device you have and are especially great at producing dark French and Spanish roasts. They'll also work better for some beans than others. Smaller beans don't roast especially well with this method; this includes several Yemeni varieties, as well as Hawaiian Maui and Kona beans. Peaberries, on the other hand, work especially well in stovetop roasters because they roll easily against the base of the drum.

The advantage of a stovetop popper is that it is relatively quiet, making it easier to hear the first and second crack. You also get complete control over the length of the roast and the amount of heat that you're applying, although it will also take some practice to find the right heat level. Roasting with a stovetop popper does produce quite a bit of smoke, and takes a bit more effort than other roasting methods since you have to crank the handle continuously to keep the beans from burning. This cranking will get easier as the roast goes on and the individual beans lose density, but you will need to do it continuously.

You can use either a gas or an electric burner for roasting with a stovetop popper. Use either a low flame or a medium burner setting. Never use high heat; this may burn the coffee, and almost invariably will mean the coffee roasts too quickly. Heat up the popper until the thermometer reads a temperature of 400°F on the interior. At this point pour in your beans and start steadily turning the crank. The temperature will vary as you continue the cooking process, but you should try to keep it from dropping below 350°F or rising above 500°F. If the crank ever starts to stick, don't force it; just turn it back the other way until it loosens and starts turning easily again.

It takes a bit longer to roast with a stovetop popper than an air popper—around 9-12 minutes, depending on the level of roast. You should hear the first crack at around 6 minutes in. Once the first crack wraps up, start checking on the color of the beans more frequently, every 30 seconds or so. The shape of the stovetop roaster means opening it to visually check the beans will release some heat, making it especially valuable to develop the skill of roasting by sound and smell only so you can maintain the temperature inside the roasting chamber.

Oven roasting

If you don't want to buy any extra equipment at all, you can even roast beans in your oven. This method will be the hardest to control and is typically not able to produce light roasts with any consistency. You also can't use this method if you have an electric oven; only a gas oven will provide an even enough cooking temperature for quality roasting. The advantage, though, is that you can roast a significantly higher volume of beans in a day than with any other home method.

You can use a variety of different implements to hold the beans as you roast them. One option is to lay them out in a single layer on a baking sheet, but this will be more likely to make them scorch on one side from the direct contact with the metal. Getting a steamer tray and placing it on the baking sheet before putting the beans down will allow more air to pass over the beans, resulting in a more even roast. You can also use a metal colander to facilitate airflow.

Start by preheating your oven to 500°F. Use a thermometer to make sure that the oven is truly up to temperature before you put the beans in. Place them on the middle rack of the oven. After around 5-7 minutes you should hear the first crack. Wait another couple of minutes after this to start checking the beans for color. If your oven doesn't have a window and you have to open the door, do it as quickly as possible and only open it a crack so that the heat doesn't escape. Like with other methods, you want to pull the beans out of the oven when they're a slightly paler color than what you're looking for.

Oven roasting is slower than other methods—around 12-15 minutes, all told. If the roast takes longer than 20 minutes to complete, the beans will taste flat and stale. If this is the case, turn the temperature up to 520°F the next time you roast, and try to avoid opening the oven door to check the colors any more than strictly necessary.

Timing is the Key

As was mentioned before, coffee beans need some time to vent the gasses that build up inside them during roasting. Trying to grind and brew beans directly from the roaster will often end up making quite the mess, as the gaseous grinds make the water bubble up and over the brewer. Whether you're buying them from a local roaster or roasting them yourself at home, you want to give the beans between 12 and 24 hours to vent off any remaining carbon dioxide before you give them a taste.

Having said that, however, you also don't want to wait too long. Most beans will be at their peak of freshness between one and five days after they're roasted, though others will maintain their best flavors up to two weeks after the roast date. You can help to keep the beans as fresh as possible as long as possible by storing them correctly. Once the gasses have vented, you want to keep the roasted beans in an airtight container that's away from moisture and out of direct sunlight. It's also best not to store these beans in the fridge or freezer, both to maintain the proper moisture content and because coffee beans tend to act like little sponges, absorbing any flavors or aromas they're exposed to.

The main advantage of roasting your own beans at home is that you'll always know exactly when they were roasted, and you'll always be guaranteed to be able to brew a fresh cup. Because of this, it often won't serve you best to roast your coffee too far ahead of time. Most people find roasting themselves a 2-3 day supply at one time gives them the ideal level of freshness, but even if your schedule only permits you to roast once a week, you'll still be fairly guaranteed to have fresher beans than you'd get going to your local roaster.

Roasting coffee is both a science and an art. Doing it well means developing a feel for it, one that you can often only get through frequent practice and experimentation. Even the fanciest and most expensive roasters with the largest array of settings won't save you if you don't know how to roast the coffee properly. Learning the craft, on the other hand, means that you won't need to spend a bunch of money on a top-notch roaster to get the best flavor out of your beans.

JESSICA SIMSS

Brewing and Grinding Coffee

How to Make Good Coffee at Home

JESSICA SIMSS

Mr. Coffee machine

For most casual coffee drinkers, when you think about brewing the first picture that pops into your head is probably the ubiquitous Mr. Coffee machine, or else perhaps the large espresso machines you'll see used in cafes. Both of these are actually relatively recent additions to the coffee brewer's arsenal, compared to the centuries-long history of the beverage—and there are a plethora of other brewing options out there in the world, many of which are very easy and affordable to bring into your own home.

The flavors within a coffee bean are complex, developed over the life of the bean. From the climate where it's grown to the way it's picked and processed to the level of roasting it undergoes, everything that's done to a bean will be designed to bring out certain flavors characteristics. The way that the beans are then brewed into a beverage will determine which of those flavors are most dominant in the cup.

In The Perfect Cup by Timothy Castle, he uses the development of a photograph as an analogy for brewing coffee. In a picture, the subject of the photo is unchanging once you snap the shutter, but there's a lot of latitude in the dark room for how you interpret that shot, choosing which elements you want to emphasize and which to obscure. If you think of the bean as your subject, the brewing method is your dark room, where you can choose how you want to interpret the bean's potential to best suit your own palate.

There is no such thing as an objectively perfect cup of coffee. As with all matters of taste, what coffee should be is up to the opinion of the drinker. The texture can be thin like tea or thick and viscous; the notes can range from fruity and flowery to deep roasted and dark chocolate bitter flavors. All of these are acceptable if they're the taste you're looking for.

When picking your beans, the most important thing to look for across the board is freshness. If they're vacuum-sealed, you can consider them fresh for up to a week after you break the seal, regardless of their roast date. If air can reach the beans, however, you'll want to make sure the roast date is indicated on the bag, and that you use them up within two weeks of this benchmark. Beyond this, the differences between roast levels and growing regions will be largely subjective, and though there are certain cultivars and regions generally regarded as superior by the specialty coffee community, these aren't necessarily the right coffees for you.

Choosing the right beans is the first step toward getting your perfect cup of coffee, but changing your brewing method can help you to further customize the experience. The chapters that follow in this book will explore a variety of popular brewing methods in detail, starting with the best-known and moving on to some that you may not have experienced as of yet. Brewing coffee is both an art and a science. To get it right, you need to understand what causes certain flavors to come out in the brew—and then practice doing it until you can consistently recreate the same cup, time after time. This book will fill in the knowledge side of that; the practicing part of it is up to you.

Brewing Basics

Brewing coffee is both an art and a science. The basic concept is simple: put ground coffee beans into contact with water, which will then extract compounds from the beans that imbue the water with the flavor elements we know as brewed coffee. The artistry comes into play in the details. The size of the grind, the length of the brew, and the method of extraction will all play a part in which flavor notes are emphasized in the final cup.

The coffee brewing process can be broken down into three general stages. The first is the wetting, when the grounds are saturated, releasing trapped carbon dioxide and making the coffee bubble up; this stage is also referred to as the "bloom." The second is the dissolution when the dissolvable solids in the coffee are extracted. Finally, there's the diffusion, when these dissolved solids spread outward into the remainder of the water. The dissolution and the diffusion stages are often lumped together under the umbrella term "extraction."

The degree of the extraction is primarily determined by the relationship between two factors: the size of the grind and the contact time between the grinds and the water. The shorter the contact time, the more finely the coffee should be ground to reach the same level of extraction. This is why fast brewing methods like espresso use a very fine grind, while longer processes like French press or cold brew use a coarse grind.

The main principle you want to keep in mind when you're brewing is to keep the best and leave the rest. The ultimate goal is to extract all the flavor compounds and oils containing the flavors you want in your cup and avoid extracting the elements you don't. While there are some notes that are generally considered to be more desirable than others, which flavors are desirable is a matter of your personal taste. Beyond this, there are a few general tips you can apply to your coffee brewing to get a consistently good flavor, whatever notes you're looking for:

Keep your equipment clean.

Dirty equipment can give your coffee a strange aftertaste. The oils in coffee do eventually go bad, and if they're allowed to sit for too long, this gives your brewed coffee stale or even rancid notes. This applies to your brewer, of course, but also make sure you're keeping your grinder clean, especially if you use a burr grinder, which is known to trap small coffee particles.

Use good water.

The beverage that ends up in your cup is between 98% and 99% water. If this water has a lot of sediment or an odd taste, this will carry through into the final brew. Filtered water is best. Naturally, soft water will give you the best brew, but artificially softened water will yield the worst, giving even the best beans a flat taste. Make sure the water is cold when you put it in the kettle or reservoir to heat it; water that has been pre-heated or has gone through the water heater will have a similar flat, stale taste to hard water.

Brew the right amount.

This applies firstly to the ratio of water to coffee, which needs to be correct for the brewing level to get the best taste in your cup. It also applies to how much total coffee you brew, however. You want to strive to brew just as much as you want to drink, just before you want to drink it. Coffee that cools and is re-heated will lose a lot of its flavor, while coffee that's allowed to sit on the "keep warm" burner will start to pick up burnt, carbon notes the longer it's left heating, destroying whatever good flavors you'd had in it.

Use good beans.

Certain brewing methods may be better at bringing out certain flavors than others, but no brewing method will be able to add notes to a coffee that weren't there to begin with. If the beans are stale, low-quality, or poorly roasted, the best you can hope to do with the brewing is cover up the bad tastes; you won't be able to make it any better than the potential in the bean.

Be consistent.

The same beans brewed in the same method can taste drastically different if you're not consistent with your water to coffee ratio, your grind level, and your brew time. Being consistent will let you troubleshoot the off flavors more effectively, figuring out where they came from and removing them the next time. It also makes sure that you can replicate the same flavor every time once you find the coffee you're looking for.

Coffee accessories

The first accessory you think about when you consider brewing coffee is the coffee filter. Not all brewing methods will use these, but they're integral to brewing methods like drip, pour over, and Aeropress, and just like anything else that comes into contact with the coffee while you're brewing it, will have an impact on the ultimate flavor.

The traditional filter for both drip and pour over is made of paper. These are traditionally made out of thin, white paper, though this practice has come under criticism in recent years because of the chemicals used to bleach the paper, mainly Dioxin, which is classified as a carcinogen by the EPA. While tests conducted by the EPA showed there were no significant quantities of dioxin in coffee brewed using paper filters, for some people simply the risk of exposure is enough to make them seek other options.

You can find "natural" paper filters that are unbleached for all the standard filter sizes, though you may need to purchase them through online retailers instead of in your local grocery store. These natural filters have their own issues, however. They can give the coffee a distinctive, cardboard-like aftertaste, especially when the coffee itself is relatively mild and subtle. There is also some small amount of bleaching that still has to happen to meet the minimum standards for paper, so you may not be saving yourself as much exposure to chemicals as you would think.

You can also go the route of a re-usable metal mesh filter. These are a larger initial investment but will last for years, saving you money in the long run. They also cut down significantly on the amount of waste associated with brewing coffee. The small gaps in the metal mesh allow more oils and other flavor compounds to get through into the brew than a paper filter does, so the coffee brewed using these filters will have a slightly stronger, darker taste with a fuller texture, and you may need to adjust your brewing techniques accordingly.

There are two other pieces of equipment that should be considered necessities for most brewing methods: a kettle and a kitchen scale.

Automatic brewers with built-in reservoirs (like espresso machines or drip machines) will not require kettles, but for the rest, you'll need some way to heat the water. If you mostly brew using French press or Aeropress, you can get any style of stovetop or electric kettle capable of heating water to boiling. If you plan to do pour-over or Chemex brewing, though, you'll want a more specialized model known as a gooseneck kettle. These are available in both stovetop and electric versions, and though they cost a bit more on average, getting an even, consistent pour is much more difficult without one.

Regardless of your brewing method, weighing your beans is a far more accurate way to measure their quantity than using a volume measurement like a tablespoon. Coffee beans grown in different climates and elevations will naturally have different densities; these differences are furthered by the roast level. An ounce of a light-roasted Peaberry takes up less space than an ounce of an Italian roast, for example. If you don't have a kitchen scale already and want to tailor your purchase specifically to coffee, look for one that's large enough to accommodate your brewer, in terms of both its dimensions and the weight it can bear. Precision is important, too. Most coffee recipes and ratios will be given in grams, and being able to weigh in tenths of a gram will give you the most accurate brew.

You may find it helpful to keep a dedicated kitchen timer for brewing, but this is increasingly less important in the era of iPhones and Alexa. While it's very important to time your brews, the source of the timer isn't important. Truly dedicated coffee connoisseurs will also keep a thermometer on hand to test the temperature of their water throughout the brewing process. A thermometer can be extremely helpful in identifying problems with the brew, but so long as you're using water that's fresh off of boiling, it will be hot enough to extract the flavors from your coffee.

Grinding Basics

If there is one phase of the brewing process where more damage can be done to the bean's flavors than any other, it's the grinding stage. Grinding at the wrong time, or to the wrong grain size for the brew method, can obscure or even eliminate some of the best flavors of the beans.

To understand why this requires some knowledge of where coffee's flavor comes from. What we think of as simply something's "flavor" is actually a combination of both its taste and its aroma. Think about how different things taste when you have a stuffy nose. A lot of flavors that we assume come from our tongues—including many fruity flavors, which are big aspects of coffee—actually come from our noses.

When it comes to coffee, the actual "taste" of it comes from non-volatile compounds like carbohydrates, caffeine, and certain acids. These bring flavors you'd describe as roasted or bitter, like nut or chocolate notes, and also contribute a lot to the coffee's texture and body. The "aroma," meanwhile, comes from a combination of volatile chemicals like alcohols and esters, and provides many of the most desired flavors in the cup.

These volatile compounds start to escape from the bean once it's roasted. Most coffee beans hit their peak freshness around 48 hours after roasting. They'll retain enough of these compounds to still be considered fresh up to around two weeks after the roast date, but after that, they'll begin to taste flat and stale. Exposure to the open air increases the rate of flavor loss; storing your beans in an airtight container will help to slow it by limiting the oxidation of the bean.

Grinding the coffee does the opposite. When the beans are ground, their surface area increases dramatically, and the physical structures that were trapping gasses and other volatile compounds are shattered. Within 15 minutes of grinding, up to half of the coffee's aromatics are lost. The single most important thing you can do to improve your home-brewed cup is to grind your coffee at home immediately before brewing it. If you've been buying pre-ground coffee, making this simple switch will have an instant impact, bringing a brightness and complexity to the finished cup you might not even have realized was missing before.

There is an incredibly wide array of coffee grinders out there. They can cost anywhere from ten bucks to a couple hundred dollars and can generally be broken down into two categories based on the mechanism used to grind the beans: burr grinders and blade grinders.

Burr grinders

The burr mill or burr grinder is not a tool unique to coffee. It is used to describe any grinder which uses two rotating abrasive surfaces to grind food. The traditional design of a burr mill uses a hand crank, which is serviceable if you're only grinding a few teaspoons of spice for a recipe, but far more tedious when you're grinding several ounces worth of coffee. While you can find manual coffee grinders, the majority of burr grinders are at the very least electric, with higher-end models offering various degrees of automation.

The burrs in a coffee grinder are typically steel discs with diagonal ridges along the facing edges. They can be cylindrical (where the two burrs are concentric circles) or conical (where the center burr is cone-shaped and the other one surrounds it). If you take the hopper off of a burr grinder and look down inside it, you'll be able to see what style of burr it uses. Adjusting the grind setting changes the distance between the burrs, in turn changing the size of the particles coming out the other side.

The consistency of the grind is the main advantage with burr grinders. The beans are crushed between the burrs and then sent down a chute into some kind of catch or receptacle, and since all the pieces pass through the same sized space for roughly the same amount of time, they all come out to be very close to the same size and shape. You can also make very fine and accurate adjustments with a burr grinder. Putting it on a certain setting will give you the same grind size every single time you use it, with no guessing.

The main disadvantage of a burr grinder is the cost. You should expect to spend between $50 and $100 for a dependable burr grinder for most home coffee brewing. If you're looking for a grinder with the precision to brew quality espresso, they can cost $200 or more. They are also significantly larger and heavier than most blade grinders and can be more complicated to maintain and repair. If you're looking to upgrade your coffee drinking experience, however, upgrading from a blade to a burr grinder will undeniably improve the taste of your cup.

Blade grinders

This is the more common style of grinder in most American households. They're typically cylindrical, as opposed to the hourglass design of the burr grinder. The coffee beans are placed into a chamber with a pair of propeller-like blades that rotate at high speed when activated; the degree of the grind is determined by how long you run the blades.

As opposed to the burr grinder, which crushes the beans, the blade grinder slices them as it spins around, going over the same pieces of beans again and again until they're the size you want them. This makes it harder to achieve consistency both within each grind and from one to the next. You can help the beans make more even contact with the blades by gently shaking it while grinding, but even still you'll have a lot of size variation, and it's almost impossible to make fine adjustments or achieve specific grinds. The blades also generate a significant amount of kinetic energy as they slice through the beans, which can start to pre-emptively heat the oils in the coffee, causing the grinds to clump and pre-emptively releasing some of the volatile aromatic compounds. Using short pulses instead of one long grind can help slow this, but at a certain grind level, it's hard to avoid.

Blade grinders have their flaws—but they're also much more affordable than burr grinders. You can get a serviceable one for as little as $10. They're also extremely easy to use and to clean and take up much less space in your kitchen. For pure taste, a burr grinder is decidedly superior, but having a blade grinder at home will still be a significant improvement over buying store-ground coffee. If you are using a blade grinder, you'll likely be best served by the more forgiving brewing methods, like drip and immersion brewing.

Espresso

No brewing method is more prescriptive and mysterious than the espresso shot. It requires a precise technique and complicated machines whose whirs and hisses can be intimidating to the non-initiated. It is unique from the other brewing methods that will be discussed in this book in a variety of ways—not least of which is the fact that it is almost exclusively brewed by professionals in coffee shops, and very rarely by the home hobbyist. But while you may not be ready to drop $1,000 on an espresso machine, understanding how espresso is made—and exactly what makes it different from other brewing methods—is perhaps the best way to understand the science behind coffee.

Espresso also produces a brew that's scientifically different than coffee brewed through other methods. Coffee made in a drip or pour over method, for example, is mostly water with some dissolved solid compounds, about 1-2% of the brew by weight. Espresso, on the other hand, is what is known as a multiphasic system. It contains dissolved solids like other coffee but also contains suspended oils and other solids, which are what give the beverage its distinctive thick texture and the cap of pale froth, known as crema, that is the hallmark of a quality espresso shot.

It should be stated that Espresso is a brewing method, not a type of bean. You'll often see the term "espresso roast" applied to coffee. This means those beans have been blended and roasted with espresso in mind, but any coffee can be brewed as espresso, and indeed the current trend in the coffee industry is toward single-origin espressos over the traditional dark-roasted blend.

There is a standard definition of espresso that has been accepted by the Specialty Coffee Association of America (SCAA) and is the formula taught to most baristas when they're first getting comfortable with an espresso machine. A single shot of espresso is defined as a one-ounce beverage brewed by passing water of between 195°F and 205°F through 9-11 grams of finely ground coffee at 9 bars of pressure for between 20 and 30 seconds. While this may seem quite technical to the layperson, the details regarding pressure, dosing, and water temperature are all important to achieving the multiphasic system that gives espresso its distinctive body.

The machine

On first glance, a professional-level espresso machine can be very intimidating. It will typically feature one to two steam wands (for frothing and heating milk) as well as one to four separate brewing stations, called groups. Each of these will have a removable brewing basket with a handle, called a portafilter, which is filled with coffee then inserted back into the group head. Metal mesh diffuser screens screwed onto the group heads filter the grinds and prevent them from being sucked up into the inner workings of the machine. When the brew is started, water is pulled through the boiler, flash heated, and then forced through the tightly-packed grounds at a high level of pressure.

Semi-automatic espresso machines are the most common. These use electronics to control the water temperature and pressure; the barista presses a button to start the brew, and even if there is an option to stop after a certain time, often have the option to manually control the length of the shot. A manual espresso machine, on the other hand, requires the barista to pull a lever that also gives them control over the amount of pressure used at various points during the brew. A fully automatic machine typically has a built-in hopper and controls the grind and dose as well as the shot time, water temperature, and pressure with one push of the button; these tend to be more common in larger corporate cafes, where the emphasis is on foolproof consistency more than the individual barista's artistry.

Home espresso machines will typically follow this same basic set-up on a smaller scale; fully-automatic and semi-automatic models are available in a variety of price points. The main issue with most home espresso machines (and the reason the majority are dismissed by coffee professionals) is that they don't have sufficient power to reach a full 9 bars of pressure during the brew. This leads to an under-extracted brew that's slightly stronger than typical coffee but lacks the multiphasic system that would make it true espresso. This is not true of all home machines, of course, but the ones that can make true espresso tend to be on the higher end of the cost spectrum.

Because they are also the most internally complicated brewing method, using the right water is also important when it comes to an espresso machine. Proper filtration is a necessity. Minerals and other microscopic sediments in tap water can accumulate in the tubes of the machine, clogging the system and leading to costly repairs. If you're going to invest in a home machine, it's worth it to take the extra step to remove all scale and sediment from your water.

Grind and dosing

Espresso has the shortest water contact time of any brewing method, and as a result requires an exceptionally fine grind—finer than can typically be achieved with a blade grinder. Coffee shops will often use designated grinders for their espresso, separate from the ones they use for drip or other methods, which allow a finer degree of control over the size of the grind.

The vast majority of espresso machines are designed to pour two shots at once; you'll be able to tell this is the case because the portafilter will have two spouts coming down from the base of it. If this is the case for your machine, simply double the dose of grinds, so you're using between 18 and 22 grams of coffee, which should produce two ounces of beverage. The brew time should remain the same, around 20-30 seconds, though the ideal time within that range will depend on the coffee you're brewing.

You will need a burr grinder for espresso, as was mentioned above. Blade grinders create too much heat, which can cause the coffee to clump by the time it's fine enough for you to use, which will make the extraction uneven. If you're using an all-purpose burr grinder, go with the second-finest setting, which will be labeled "espresso" on most machines. You're ultimately looking for grinds that are around the same size as table salt. While espresso-specific grinders from brands like Mahlkonig and Baratza will give you a finer degree of control over the size of the grind, the espresso setting on any burr grinder should work well enough for a home espresso maker. If your shots are brewing too quickly, your coffee is too coarse; if they're brewing too slowly, that means it's too fine. An easy way to remember this is to think about pouring water through a pile of gravel and then pouring the same amount of water through a pile of sand. The water will go through the gravel much faster than it does through the sand because the space between the larger pieces gives it more space to move.

Tamping

Tamping is a step unique to espresso brewing and is an important part of the technique. If you were to simply put loose grounds in the portafilter and try to brew without tamping, the water will flow through the coffee far too quickly, regardless of how finely you grind it. Applying pressure to the grinds condenses them to ensure an even extraction and prevent what's known as "channeling," where the water finds the path of least resistance through the grinds, over-extracting some areas and leaving others dry. This can still occur even after tamping if there are cracks in the puck from impacts against the portafilter but is far less likely if you have the right technique.

Espresso tamps are essentially weighted discs of metal attached to a handle. They come in a variety of diameters to match with different sizes of the portafilter. The standard size is 58 millimeters in diameter and this is the size most tamps are designed to accommodate. You want the tamp to fit snugly down inside the brew basket without rubbing up against the sides when you press.

The ideal tamp should apply around 30 pounds of pressure to the coffee in the portafilter; you can practice on a bathroom scale to get a sense of what this feels like. Thirty pounds of pressure is a good baseline for your tamping practice, but you should feel free to adjust the pressure to suit your grind and machine. Make sure that you're tamping straight down, with even pressure applied to all areas within the basket. If your tamp is angled or uneven, the grinds in the basket will be more compressed in some areas than others, which can lead to an uneven extraction. A tamp that's too light or too heavy can also affect the brew time of your shots. If you're relatively sure that the grind is the right size but your brew is too quick or too slow, consider changing up your tamp—less pressure to make it brew faster, and more pressure to make it brew more slowly.

Pulling shots

Many semi-automatic espresso machines will have a timer associated with each group head that you can use to track your shots; if yours doesn't, a simple kitchen timer should do the trick. Start it as soon as you press the button to begin the brew. It will normally take a few seconds for the coffee to start flowing through the spouts; this should be considered part of the brew time since the water has made contact with the coffee and the extraction has started.

If your machine allows you to manually adjust the brew temperature, this can be a fun thing to play with as you continue to perfect your shots. Even changing the temperature by a single degree can bring out different flavors from the beans. Brewing at a lower temperature will emphasize the brighter, fruitier notes of the coffee while brewing at a higher temperature will bring out more of the dark and roasted flavors of the bean.

If you pull your shots correctly, it should have two distinct layers when it finishes brewing: a dark brown liquid underneath (the shot) and a tan-colored frothy layer of about ½ inch thick on top (the crema). This crema will dissipate within a few minutes of pulling the shot, which is part of the reason espresso is typically enjoyed quickly. It is also the necessary aspect of the espresso for making latte art, and a good crema is generally accepted to be the sign of a well-pulled shot.

Cleaning an espresso machine

After every single shot that you pull, you should knock the grounds out of the portafilter and wipe out the inside of the brew basket with a dry cloth. After you've done this (and before replacing the portafilter in the group) flush the lines by running pure water through them for a second or two. Use caution when you do this, as the water will be at brewing temperature.

Professional machines are more thoroughly cleaned at least once per day. This is not necessarily for home machines as it's related more to the volume of shots pulled than the amount of time that passed since the last cleaning. A once per week cleaning routine should be fine for daily espresso drinkers; if you use your machine less often than this, you can change your cleaning schedule accordingly.

You can find espresso machine cleaner either online or at a well-stocked café. Look for something called Cafiza; this is what the professionals use, and is excellent for removing the oils and gunk from coffee that can build up in your machine. Your machine should come with a "blind," which is a brew basket with a solid bottom that you can insert in the portafilter for cleaning. This process is also referred to by baristas as "backflushing" because it involves using the pressure of the machine to foam the cleaner and flush it back through the tubes of your machine.

Put a dime-sized pile of Cafiza powder in the blind portafilter and start the brew. Do 10 seconds on followed by 10 seconds off; repeat four or five times. When you're finished, carefully remove the portafilter and dump it, then run clean water through the group to remove any extra in the lines. Finally, unscrew the diffuser screen and give it a good scrub, checking for any coffee particles that have worked their way in under the screen.

Drip Brewing

The drip brewer is the most popular brewing method in the United States, largely because of its low cost and high convenience. Brewing a cup on drip takes longer than many other brewing methods—around six to eight minutes on average—but you don't have to stand there and keep an eye on the brew while it's happening; simply put grinds in the filter and water in the reservoir and hit start, and you can walk away and finish your morning routine. The warmer on the machine will even keep the coffee hot if you can't get to it right away.

Drip machines are the only widely available brewers for the home consumer that come with automation features, as well. Many drip machines that you can buy in the department store can be programmed to start brewing at a certain time, though you'll likely need to prepare them with ground coffee and water manually ahead of time. This makes them perfect for busy mornings at home, as well as for offices and other settings where different people may be brewing the coffee.

The general idea behind drip brewing is to pour near-boiling water slowly over and through the grounds, which are contained in a filter in the brew basket of the machine. This gives it a longer water contact time than methods like espresso and pour over but not quite as long of a contact time as immersion brewing methods. In the standard drip machine, there will be a reservoir that you fill manually with water along the back of the machine. This is drawn automatically through the machine, where it's heated to between 195°F and 205°F before being passed over the grounds in the brew basket. The amount of water and grounds that you put into the machine will determine the amount of coffee that is brewed, as well as the strength of the beverage.

You may hear coffee experts downplaying the quality of coffee that's produced in a drip method, but this has less to do with the brewing than with the quality level of cheaply made drip machines. Many cheap drip machines do not actually reach the temperature of 195°F, resulting in the brew being under-extracted. Some drip machines also take too long to brew. The total brew time using a drip method should be between five and seven minutes; longer than this, and the resulting beverage may taste over-extracted and weak. The "keep warm" burner under the pot can also burn the coffee if it's left sitting on it too long, also contributing to the reputation of drip coffee as inferior. The truth is, however, that if you buy a quality drip machine, it will give you coffee equal in quality to what you'd get from any other brewing method.

The most highly-touted drip machines do not come cheaply. Among these are models from Bonavita and the Moccamaster line from Technivorm, each of which will cost you a couple hundred dollars. This does not mean that you have to spend hundreds of dollars to get a decent drip machine, however; while not every $20 coffee maker will reach the right temperature and brew time, you can find relatively inexpensive drip coffee makers that will give you a delicious cup of coffee.

Regardless of what kind of drip machine you have, one trick that can help is to pre-wet the coffee before you start the brew. To do this, boil a small amount of water in a kettle and sprinkle it over the grinds in the filter just before you start the brew. This will jump-start the extraction process, pulling the oils to the surface so you get more intense flavors. This can be an especially useful technique if you're only making a small amount of coffee, which may cut the water contact time short.

Filters

The shape of your brew basket will determine what kind of filter you need to use for your drip machine. The two most common shapes are flat-bottomed (the cylindrical shape with the scalloped edges you're likely most familiar with) and cone-shaped, which is the same general size and shape as a pour over filter.

Most people choose to go with a paper filter when they're brewing drip. These filters are single-use and can be disposed of with the grinds after each batch that you brew. You can also buy reusable wire mesh filters of both common shapes, which you empty and then rinse after each brew. Paper filters will give you a slightly cleaner cup, as more of the coffee oils can get through a wire mesh filter than a paper one. In terms of comparison with other brewing methods, a paper filter will give you a taste more similar to that of pour over, while re-usable metal filters will give you a brew that tastes more like a French press.

Grind and dosage

The style of filter that your machine uses will determine the correct grind for your brew. If you're using a flat-bottomed filter, use the #6 setting on a burr grinder; this may also be labeled as "drip" or "auto-drip." If you're using a cone filter, you'll want to make the grind a bit finer—the #4 setting on a burr grinder, which may be labeled "fine" or "medium-fine," depending on the grinder.

Because it's a fairly forgiving brewing method, drip machines are some of the few that can still give you a great cup without a burr grinder. If you're using a blade grinder, you'll probably want to stick to paper filters instead of mesh, or you may find a lot of fines in your cup. Go with a medium grind, or around 20-25 seconds total in short bursts.

Either way, you grind it, you'll want to use around 10-12 grams of coffee for every cup of water. Using a kitchen scale to weigh the beans will give you the most consistently accurate cup, but you can approximate the right amount by using two level tablespoons. After you've poured the grounds into the filter, give it a little shake to even out the surface; this will help them to extract evenly.

Best coffees for drip

The drip method works well with a wide range of coffee origins and grind levels, from the brightest, fruitiest light roast to the deepest, most chocolatey dark roast. This makes it one of the most versatile brewing methods. More subtle flavor characteristics may not come out as prominently in a drip machine as with manual brewing. Turn to drip when you're looking for a balanced cup, regardless of the roast level of the beans.

Cleaning drip machines

The per-batch clean-up for a drip machine is relatively simple and straightforward. Simply remove the filter from the brew basket and deposit the grounds into the trash, then rinse out the coffee pot before returning it to the machine. Depending on how frequently you use your drip machine, you'll want to perform a more thorough cleaning every one to three months. You can buy specific solutions designed to remove coffee oils and built-up grinds from the machine. Alternatively, you can brew a mixture of diluted vinegar through the machine, then follow this with three to four passes with pure water to avoid having an acidic taste in your next pot.

Pod brewers

One popular modern take on the drip machine is the pod brewer, known colloquially as a K-Cup machine or a Keurig, after the brand that popularized the method. In these machines, the coffee is pre-weighed into single-serving pods, which are then brewed in a method fairly similar to what happens in a drip coffee maker. Convenience is the main selling point of these machines. The consumer doesn't have to think about grinding or dosing, and the entire brewing process lasts no longer than two minutes.

Most serious coffee drinkers denounce pod brewers, and with good reason. The fatal flaw of most of these devices is that the boilers are too small to heat the water enough for successful extraction. When tested, no pod brewer currently on the market registered a brew temperature higher than 193°F. Combined with the short water contact time, this inevitably results in a weak, under-extracted brew.

The pods themselves have their own array of issues. The coffee inside them is not only ground weeks or even months before brewing, it is often degassed prior to packaging, meaning it's lost most of its volatile aromas before it even leaves the factory. Pods also cost between three and five times as much per cup compared to other brewing methods, meaning you're paying a fortune for stale coffee.

If you already have a pod machine, you can defray the cost (and save some flavor) by purchasing a reusable pod filter. You can then use any coffee in it that you want. Grind the beans the same way you would for a cone drip filter (medium-fine to fine). It will still suffer from under-extraction, so bold, medium-roasted coffees will give you the best results. If you're in the market for a new brewer, however, steer clear of pod brewers. Until the method is improved, it sacrifices too much flavor for the sake of convenience.

Pour Over and Chemex

When people talk about "manual brewing methods," nine times out of ten they're referring to the pour over method. It uses the same basic concept as a drip machine, using a similar grind size, though a slightly shorter water contact and brew time. The main difference is that with pour over and Chemex brewing the user is responsible for pouring the water and timing the brew as opposed to the automated process of the machine. This means you can guarantee an even extraction across the grounds and adjust the level and speed of the water accordingly to give yourself the ideal cup for your tastes.

As opposed to the immersion brewing methods that will be discussed in the next two chapters, the water in a pour over method is replenished continuously throughout the brew cycle. This makes for a more aggressive extraction, as fresh water is constantly coming into contact with the exterior of the grounds. This is the reason it requires a shorter brew time. If you were to continue pouring water for the 6-8 minutes of a drip brew cycle, it would result in an over-extracted beverage.

Pour over is one of the least intrusive and least expensive methods you can use to brew coffee. The pour over brewer is basically a cone of plastic, glass, or ceramic that you set directly on top of the cup or vessel you're brewing into. You can buy a plastic model for as little as $10; glass or ceramic models may cost as much as $25. Plastic tends to be the most durable, though ceramic and glass models will give you more consistent heat retention throughout the brew.

Chemex brewers use the same concept, though the vessel contains both the brewing cone and the serving vessel in one piece. They also tend to cost a bit more—between $30 and $50, depending on the size of the flask. This extra cost is largely because of their aesthetic appeal. The design of the Chemex brewer is beautiful enough that there's one on permanent display at the Museum of Modern Art in New York City; it is equally appealing on the center of your table at a dinner party, and the manual brewing method is likely to impress your guests. All Chemex flasks are made of the same borosilicate glass on the interior; any wooden aspects of the design are purely aesthetic.

Necessary accessories

Pour over brewing traditionally uses paper filters, of a similar style and shape to what you'd use for cone-shaped brew baskets in drip machines. These cost around $5-$10 for a pack of 100 filters and can be inserted directly into the brewer out of the package. You could also use a gold mesh filter if you want a more environmentally-friendly brewing option. As with drip brewing, changing the filter style will change the taste slightly, with the wire mesh filter allowing more of the coffee oils to extract into the beverage.

Chemex brewers, on the other hand, use their own proprietary filters. These are made of a paper-like material that's unbleached and thicker than the standard coffee filter you're accustomed to from the grocery store. This added substance to the filter is one of the main reasons Chemex brewing produces such a clean cup of coffee. You can buy different styles of Chemex filter, some of which are semi-circular and others of which are square. Some of these will also require folding before being placed into the brewer. Exactly which filter you need will depend on which size of Chemex you own.

While filters are the only absolutely necessary additional supplies for brewing with pour over, making the most of the brewing method will require something slightly more sophisticated than your standard water pitcher or tea kettle. The way the water moves inside a standard teapot's spout makes it very difficult to control and limit the flow throughout the brew. This will result in some areas getting more water than others, which will ultimately result in uneven extraction and a less flavorful cup. You'll have much better luck if you use a gooseneck kettle. These are named for the slender, long, and curving spout attached to these kettles. The extra length helps to regulate the flow of water so it comes out with the same force regardless of how much water is inside. You can get stovetop or electric versions; they will cost you around the same amount as a standard teakettle.

Grind and dose

When it comes to the amount and fineness of the grinds, pour over is in many respects the polar opposite of espresso. Rather than having a very prescriptive and limiting set of guidelines that define the proper brewing method, pour over is almost infinitely customizable, letting you make adjustments to suit your own personal tastes as the beans that you're using.

When you're first starting out, however, you may find yourself with an embarrassment of options and unsure of where to start off. A good rule of thumb is to use a ratio of 2 grams of coffee for every ounce of water. This would mean using around 32 grams of coffee for your typical "medium" cup of coffee.

In terms of the grind level, most people use a #6 setting on a burr grinder (the same one you would use for cone-shaped drip filters, often labeled as medium-fine or fine). Because of the relatively quick extraction time, it's generally recommended to use a burr grinder, but the brewing method is fairly forgiving and this is not strictly required.

Pour over techniques

The steps of the pour over method are typically just as customizable to your needs as the grind and ratio, but there are a typical order and pattern that most baristas follow, at least while they're still perfecting their technique. Heat the water while you're grinding the beans. Place the filter in the brewer, wetting it with some of the hot water as soon as it stops boiling. This both starts to heat the vessel and prevents air pockets from developing between the filter and sides of the cone, which can negatively impact the extraction.

Now you can pour your grinds into the filter. Smooth it out so the surface is relatively level and put a small divot in roughly the center of the cone. At this point, you're ready to start adding water. Begin a timer as soon as you start pouring, targeting the divot in the center then working out and back in concentric circles. Pour for around 15 seconds, then wait for 15 seconds. Repeat this pattern (15 seconds on, 15 seconds off) until your cup is full. The total brew time should end up around three to four minutes.

Clean up is a breeze with a pour-over or Chemex, too, another benefit of the method. Simply dump the filter and included grinds into the trash and give the entire brewer a good rinse with warm, soapy water. While the ridges on a pour over cone may be tricky to clean around, the interior of the Chemex doesn't have any nooks or crannies where grinds and gunk can hide, unlike a drip machine or French press.

Best coffee options

Baristas love to pour over coffee because it makes a very strong and complex brew with relatively little effort. You can use it to make any style of coffee, although the ones that will receive the most benefit are those that are difficult to perfect with other brewing methods. This includes coffees with subtle floral notes, or those with a brighter, fruity character that might get obscured in a longer brew, like a drip or French press. Coffees from Kenya and Ethiopia tend to taste especially great as a pour over, as do Central American coffees, like those from Costa Rica, Guatemala, or El Salvador.

Chemex is best-suited to a similar array of coffees. The specialized material used for the filters will give you an even cleaner and more subtle cup than standard pour over, removing many of the darker roast notes of the beans. You'll likely also find that Chemex brewing gives you a smoother and less acidic version of the coffee brewed in it, even compared to the other pour over methods.

French Press

French presses are the second-most-popular brewing method in the American kitchen following the drip method. Again, this popularity is based largely on three factors: availability, affordability, and convenience. You can buy a French press at most kitchen supply and department stores, and they come in a wide array of different sizes. Most use a glass beaker with a plastic lid and metal plunger, but you can also find all-plastic models (great if you're clumsy or plan to take it traveling) and all-metal varieties that make attractive tabletop serving vessels, as well. You may also see them sold under different names, the most common of which is a coffee press or cafetiere; you may also see it called a Melior brewer, after a brand of French presses that was popular in the 1980s and 1990s.

The design of the French press is very simple and hasn't changed much since its invention in the 1920s. You also won't need a whole host of extra accessories to make a good French press brew. While you may want to have a wooden spoon or stirrer on-hand to agitate the grinds, you don't need any filters or a specialized kettle. Aside from the occasional replacement of the beaker or filter due to wear and tear, there are no extra costs associated with French press brewing aside from the coffee itself.

The coffee grounds in a French press spend most of the brewing process in direct contact with the water. The plunging process also uses a metal as opposed to a paper filter. Similar to other metal filter and direct contact methods, this allows more of the extracted oils to brew into the beverage, resulting in a full-bodied cup that tends to have a thicker body and texture than other brewing methods, with a mouth-feel that's almost syrupy. This can be jarring if you're accustomed to the milder taste of a drip or Chemex brew but is ideal for people who like their coffee strong.

French press brewing is an excellent way to get a complex cup with minimal effort. Though you can agitate the grinds during the brewing process if you want to accelerate the extraction, you can also leave it to brew on its own while you go about the rest of your morning routine, making it basically as easy a brewing method as drip. It is also less finicky than many other brewing methods, more forgiving of issues with the grind or beans, and is an excellent brewing method for darker roasts, especially those from Brazil, Mexico, and Indonesia.

Grind and dose

The exact right grind level for French press varies depending on who you talk to. Most people favor a coarse grind, though you can utilize any grind level from coarse to medium. The smaller the grind, the more likely you'll have small coffee particles (called fines) that slip through the mesh filter and into the brew. Adherents of the French press brew consider this to be just a part of the experience, but those who aren't accustomed to the method may find it initially disconcerting.

Because it is more forgiving, French press is one of the brewing methods that works the best for those who only have a blade grinder. Start with a relatively coarse grind (the "coarse" or "French press" setting on a burr grinder, or a few short pulses with a blade grinder). If it tastes weak, use a finer grind next time; if you get acrid, bitter, over-extracted flavors, make it coarser on your next pass. In terms of the dosage, you generally want to use around a gram of coffee for every ounce of water.

Brewing method

The technique of brewing French press is very simple. Start by boiling your water and grinding your coffee. Use a bit of boiling water to warm up the press, swirling it around the sides then dumping it out. Now add your grinds to the bottom, start your timer, and gently pour in the water, making sure to saturate all the grinds and leave no dry spots. Some of the grinds will float, forming a crust on the top of the brew. When the timer reaches one minute, use a wooden spoon or paddle to break this crust, then stir the grinds until most of them are sinking instead of floating. The more you stir, the more you'll speed up the extraction, so if you want more light, bright notes use your spoon gently and sparingly.

There are two schools of thought when it comes to adding the water. Some people will suggest adding all the water at the start of the brew. Others put in half the water at the start of the brew and add the rest after they break the crust and stir. Adding the water all at once at the beginning will give you a more gradual, even extraction over the course of the brew. Replenishing the water after the first minute will speed the extraction, and is recommended mostly if you like deeper, thicker coffees.

Put the lid on the pot once you're done stirring, but don't push down the plunger yet; for the rest of the brew, the lid is just to keep the heat inside the brewing vessel. Most people recommend a four-minute brew for French press. If you like a deeper, darker brew, you can let it go longer; the grinds typically won't start to over-extract until you pass the eight-minute mark.

Once you're satisfied with the level of the brew, slowly push the plunger down with a steady, even pressure. Agitating the grinds too much at this point will start to extract undesirable stewy or carbon flavors. If the plunger catches, don't force it; just go back up a couple inches to free whatever's caught and then keep going. You can serve straight from the press, but if you're not going to drink the entire pot right away you may want to pour it into a carafe. The thin glass wall of a French press isn't great at retaining heat, and the continued contact with the grounds—though limited—will affect the flavor of the last cup.

Cleaning and maintenance

While the French press is extremely convenient in the preparation stage, it is conversely one of the trickier brewing devices to clean. This is mostly because the ground coffee is not contained in a filter, allowing every interior surface to come into contact with it. In an ideal world, you would be able to remove the filter from the plunger portion of the press and clean it after every use. At the very least, you should dump the used coffee grounds and rinse both the plunger and the interior of the beaker with hot, soapy water as soon as you've finished using it.

If oils and small coffee particles build up on the plunger this can affect the taste of your future brews, giving them an over-extracted edge or even making them taste slightly rancid. You can use any coffee maker cleaner designed for drip machines to remove these stubborn oils. Urnex is a popular brand, and Cafiza (for espresso machines) would work for this as well. Sprinkle a bit in the bottom of a large bowl then dissolve it in enough hot water to completely cover the pieces. Let it soak for a few hours, then scrub and rinse each piece and reassemble.

The sizing of French presses is standardized within brands, but not necessarily across the industry; keep that in mind if you need to buy replacement parts. If you break the glass beaker, you can get a replacement for around $5-$10, depending on the brand and capacity of your press. You can also get replacement screens for the plunger. Over time, small particles will inevitably work their way under the screen, which can also give you the over-extracted or rancid flavors mentioned above. There's no strict timeline for how often you need to replace the screen, but if it's starting to look puckered or warped, it's probably time for a new one.

Other Immersion Brewers

Immersion brewing is conceptually the simplest of the brewing methods, and was the only way to brew coffee for the first few centuries of its history. Soak ground coffee in hot water; that's really all there is to it. This makes it a more fool-proof brewing method than more complicated techniques like espresso or pour-over. The main details you need to focus on are the contact time of the water with the grounds, the size of the grind, and the ratio of coffee to water.

The French press is the most popular immersion brewer, but there are other options. Models that use a metal mesh filter will give you a similar cup profile to a French press brew, with a thick body and bold flavor that's well-suited to medium- and dark-roasted coffees. If you prefer a smoother, cleaner cup, you can also find immersion brewers that use a paper filter and will yield a cup more similar to a pour over. Immersion brewers can take a lot of forms, but there are two main characteristics you're looking for. First, it should have some method to control the grinds and keep them from escaping into the brewed coffee; second, the vessel itself should have good enough heat retention that it can keep the water between 195°F and 205°F for the entirety of the brew.

While it's a classic method, new twists on the immersion brewer have brought it back into vogue in specialty coffee circles. Each of the methods outlined below will have slightly different pros, cons, and brew requirements. They're certainly not the only immersion brewers on the market, but they're some of the most interesting and popular alternatives to the French press.

Clever

The Clever is a hybrid brewer that looks more like a pour over dripper. What makes it an immersion brewer is the stopper and release system at the bottom of the cone, which holds the water within it in direct contact with the ground coffee for the majority of the brew, the reason it's considered to be a full-immersion brewer.

Like pour overs, Clever brewers are durable and affordable (around $20 to $25, depending on where you buy it). It's made with lightweight BPA-free plastic and uses cone-shaped paper filters. Also similar to pour overs, the Clever is intended for single cup brewing. The release mechanism is designed to open when the brewer is set atop a vessel with roughly the diameter of a coffee mug, so unlike an Aeropress or pour over you'll want to keep it on a flat surface like a counter for the majority of the brew.

Start by putting your filter in the brewer cone. Grind between 20 and 25 grams of coffee while you heat your water. You can use a wide range of grind sizes with this method. Your best bet is to start with a medium setting (drip or auto-drip) then adjust accordingly, making it finer if the cup's too weak or coarser if it's too strong. Wet the filter first as soon as the water stops boiling. Make sure to press the release mechanism to drain this heating water before you add the grinds, then set the Clever on a flat surface; you can use the included coaster if you don't want to put it directly on the counter. Start a timer and pour in your water. If you want a faster, deeper extraction, break the crust and stir at the one minute mark; otherwise simply put the lid on to keep the heat in and let it go until the timer reaches 3:30. At this point, you can move the Clever to your mug and start it draining, a process that should take around 30 seconds.

Clean-up with the Clever is typically quite easy—simply dump the filter and rinse out the brewer. If your filter tears and grinds get down into the stopper mechanism it can prevent the brewer from working properly and be very difficult to clean out, so use caution especially if you like to stir during the brew to avoid damaging the filter. It's also not recommended to use wire mesh filters with the Clever for this reason.

Bonavita Immersion Dripper

This is another single-cup hybrid brewer and is very similar to the Clever. It uses the same cone-shaped paper filters and the same grind and dose requirements (medium grind, 20-25 grams of coffee for a 16-ounce cup). Because it's made of porcelain instead of plastic it has a better heat retention and allows for a longer brew time. If you prefer a thick, strong cup, this will be easier to achieve with the Bonavita than the Clever. It also costs a bit more, around $40 from most retailers.

The water release on the Bonavita is controlled with a slider on the front of the brewer instead of the pressure release system of the Clever, so you can set it on top of your coffee cup for the entirety of the brew. Once you've prepped the filter and added the grinds, start your timer and pour about half your water into the brewer. Let it bloom for 30 seconds then stir until the coffee is completely saturated. Add the rest of your water then cover to retain the heat. The drip-out process for the Bonavita takes longer than it does with the Clever, so you'll want to open the release valve when the timer hits 2:30; the brew should finish around the four-minute mark.

Sowden Softbrew

Immersion brewers that can make multiple cups at once more typically follow the carafe design of the French press than the cone-shaped design of the hybrid brewers above. The Sowden Softbrew system is one popular variant on the multi-cup immersion brewer, as renowned for the aesthetics of the carafe design as it is for the taste of the coffee it makes. It comes in a range of sizes with an Ikea-like naming system. Because the filter can be removed without draining the liquid, they're able to be used as both brewers and serving carafes, making them perfect for entertaining.

Start by grinding the coffee to a coarse or medium-coarse level (French press or the next setting up on a burr grinder) with a dose of around 60 grams of coffee for each liter of water. Put the ground coffee in the included filter basket and set it in the pot, then start your timer and pour the water in, slowly and evenly, through the grounds. Once the pot is full, cover it and allow it to steep for four minutes, then remove the filter basket. Give the coffee in the pot a good stir before serving; the more saturated coffee can sink to the bottom and give you an uneven flavor across the cups.

Sowden Softbrew uses a metal basket filter with tiny holes to allow the water to pass through and mingle with the grounds, a similar concept to the basket brewers on teapots. Though the metal filter allows for full extraction of the oils, the limited exposure of the grounds to the water makes for a cup that's thinner, smoother, and mellower than what comes out of a French press. Expect to get a lot of wonderful coffee aromas with a taste you might more readily associate with a high-end drip machine.

Solo

The Solo is another entry in the all-in-one immersion brewer category. Its hourglass shape and neoprene coating help to keep the water temperature constant throughout the brew. Like the Sowden, it uses a mesh filter to keep the grinds from slipping into the coffee, and this filter can be easily removed once the brew is done, letting you serve straight from the carafe.

Like with the Softbrew, you'll want to use a coarse or medium-coarse grind setting. Put the coffee in the filter then pour your water over it. You should see the bloom start almost instantly. If you want to agitate the grounds, do it a bit later in the process, around the two-minute mark. The brew should finish in 4-6 minutes, depending on what strength you like. Remove the filter in one smooth motion so you don't agitate the grinds too much at the end of the process.

The taste of Solo-brewed coffee is in many ways the ideal of an immersion brew. It works especially well with naturally processed coffees, bringing out complex flavor notes and giving the brew a lot of depth while still producing a generally cleaner cup than French press. The main disadvantage of the Solo is its price, which at around $80 is one of the more expensive immersion brewers on the market.

Aeropress

The Aeropress is a unique hybrid brewer that's a quick and easy way to make a cup of coffee. The short water contact time and the use of pressure to brew make it similar to an espresso brewer. The beverage it produces is more comparable to espresso than drip (for example) and it may even produce a small amount of crema, depending on the bean. There are also elements of the brew that are similar to an immersion brewer, including the agitation of the grinds and the direct contact between the grinds and the water. The look of it, meanwhile, is unique among coffee brewers—not intimidating so much as befuddling, if you've never seen one in use.

You can often find Aeropresses for sale in specialty coffee or tea shops for around $30. There's a pack of filters included, so you can use it straight out of the box. All the pieces of the machine are made of a durable BPA-free plastic that is simple to clean and virtually indestructible. Along with the brewer itself, you'll get a plastic paddle for stirring, a scoop to take the guesswork out of dosing, and a funnel for pouring in the grinds. There's even a carrying bag, in case you want to take it on the go.

Similar to pour over, the Aeropress sits directly on the mug or vessel you're brewing into. Because you'll need to be applying significant downward pressure, you should only use a sturdy, flat-bottomed vessel—nothing that's likely to tip or crack. Since it's aimed primarily at single-cup brewing, it's best to use something the size and dimensions of a ceramic coffee mug.

The paper filters that are designed for use with the Aeropress are very affordable; a pack of 350 costs around $4.50 on the Aeropress website. There are also re-usable metal options, though not as many as there are for drip machines. Able Brewing makes a stainless steel filter called the Disk. It costs $12.50 and will last for years, so if you use your Aeropress often it can be a good investment. It will also let you experiment with subtle flavor variations since the metal will allow more oils into the brew than the standard paper.

Grind and dose

The instructions that come with the Aeropress recommend using two scoops of beans ground to medium-fine per cup. If you find that the coffee you get from this tastes weak or that the water seems to be passing through the grinds too quickly or easily, you can use a smaller grind, anything up to the espresso setting on a burr grinder. It can be tricky to get your grinds to the right consistency using a blade grinder, especially if you want them on the finer side.

Brewing methods

There are two primary methods used to brew with the Aeropress: the traditional method and the inverted method. Using the traditional method will give you a beverage that's most similar in taste and texture to espresso, while the inversion method produces a cup more similar to a pour over or inversion brewer in terms of its viscosity and which notes are emphasized. If you've never used an Aeropress before, it's usually best to start with the traditional method and get used to that before trying the inverted method, which does require a bit of technique to avoid spills.

Start the traditional method by putting a filter in the perforated cap then screwing it onto the bottom of the brewer tube. Grind your coffee and heat your water. Pour a bit of hot water through the tube to wet the filter, then place it on your mug and add the coffee. Now pour in near-boiling water up to the "2" mark. A crust will quickly form on the top of the water. After a few seconds, break it and stir the grinds. Moisten the plunger to make it easier to push while you let the water sit for about ten seconds more, then insert the plunger into the top of the tube and press downward with a steady pressure. It should take you somewhere between 20 and 30 seconds to finish the plunge.

What you'll have in your cup after brewing with this method will be about the same quantity, consistency, and strength as a double shot of espresso. If you want to make a more American cup of coffee, you can dilute it water until it's your ideal strength. You can also add steamed milk to make a latte, or just drink it as-is.

The inverted method, on the other hand, treats the Aeropress more like an immersion brewer. Start by turning the Aeropress upside down, so that the end the cap screws on is facing up. Insert the plunger into the bottom just enough to seal it. This is the part of the process that many people find tricky; you may want to do it over a bowl or sink your first few times.

Because the water contact time is longer, you'll want to use a slightly coarser grind with this method—no finer than a medium, or about what you'd use for a drip machine. Grind the coffee while you boil your water, then add the coffee to the bottom of the chamber. You can experiment with the ratios, but the two scoops recommended for the traditional method is a good baseline. Start a timer when you start pouring the water in. When it reaches one minute, stir the grinds with the included paddle, agitating just enough that most of the coffee sinks.

When the timer reaches two minutes, place a filter in the cap and screw it onto the top. Gently press upwards on the plunger until a blond foam appears, then carefully turn the Aeropress over and place it on your mug. From this point, you can plunge the same way you would in the traditional method; it should take between 15 and 30 seconds.

Whichever way you use it, cleaning up after an Aeropress brew is a breeze. The plunger captures all of the coffee grounds. When you're done brewing, simply unscrew the cap and push the plunger through over your trash or compost. The filter and used coffee will pop out together in a compact puck. Rinse all the components after every use.

Best Aeropress coffees

The combination of the quick extraction and the paper filter give Aeropress coffee a smooth, mellow flavor that has strong flavor notes and a well-developed acidity. You'll find you can bring out a lot of subtle aromatic notes from natural-processed coffees, especially those from Kenya or Ethiopia. It's also a fantastic brewing method for complex bean flavors, like those from Sumatra and Papua New Guinea. You can get a smooth, almost buttery texture when you brew using Aeropress, which compliments the chocolatey and caramel notes of many high-grown South and Central American varieties, while the short brew time preserves their bright floral or fruity notes. If you like the way a coffee tastes brewed using drip or pour over, you'll probably also like it when you brew it with an Aeropress, and it will be ready to drink in about a third of the time.

Cold Brewing

If you've ever tried making your own iced coffee at home, your first inclination was probably just to brew hot coffee and then chill it, in a similar technique to what you'd use for making iced tea. The problem with this is that hot-brewed coffee's flavor changes as it cools. A lot of the brighter fruit and floral notes dissipate, leaving behind more of the dark and bitter notes, and the coffee won't be as complex or balanced by the time you drink it. Some of the acids released during hot brewing change forms as they cool, also giving coffee prepared this way a harsh, almost astringent mouth-feel.

A better alternative is to brew the coffee cold from start to finish. As with any brewing method, it will bring out different aspects of the coffee's flavor, but these flavors will be more stable and will stay preserved in the coffee until you're ready to drink it. In general, cold brewing brings out more of the rich chocolate or nut flavors from the bean and is best suited to more mild coffees where these are the predominant flavors. It works especially well with coffees from Brazil, Peru, and Colombia.

The main disadvantage of this brewing method is the length of time it takes to complete. To brew coffee at a low temperature, you need to maintain the contact of the water with the grounds for between 12 and 24 hours. This means brewing cold brew takes some advanced planning. The good news is that you can brew it in larger batches, a week's supply or more, all in one go. What you get from making cold brew will be thick and concentrated, almost more like a coffee extract. So long as it's kept in this form and in the refrigerator, it can last up to two weeks.

One other advantage of cold-brewed coffee is that it will have a lower acidity than the same bean brewed in another brewing method. Because the beans never reach a boil, some of the chemical changes that are undergone during traditional brewing don't happen, and some of those compounds are never released into the brew. This can make cold brewing a great method if you have a sensitive stomach.

Though it's only recently achieved widespread popularity, cold brew coffee is actually not new; it was popularized in the 1960s by the Toddy company, and the method they came up with is still the main one in use today. Many different coffee manufacturers have jumped on the recent cold brew trend, and you can buy smaller equivalents of the large buckets used for cold brewing at a coffee shop for use at home. While effective, these cold brew systems cost around $40, require brand-specific replacement parts and filters, and are ultimately more money than they're worth. You can just as easily make cold brew coffee in a French press. If you don't own a French press or want to make larger batches, you can make your own cold brewing system easily; both methods are outlined below.

Grind and dose

The water contact time in cold brew is longer than with any other method, and though the lack of heat does change some of the involved chemical processes, when it comes to the grind the standard principles apply. You should use the coarsest setting on a burr grinder, or just a few short pulses with a blade grinder for this method.

Since some of the flavor compounds in coffee are only brought out by heat and won't be brought out in the cold brew method, you'll need a slightly higher ratio of coffee to water than with other brewing methods. Most people recommend between a 1:3 and a 1:4 ratio of coffee to water. This means you'll use between 1/3 and ¼ lb of coffee for two liters of brew. Keep in mind, however, that the resulting brew will be a concentrate and will stretch further than the equivalent amount of hot brewed coffee.

Brewing

Cold brew is basically a very long immersion brewing process and includes most of the same steps. If you're re-purposing a French press, start by grinding the right quantity of beans for your press size, put them in the bottom of the beaker, then fill the press with filtered water. It can be any temperature from ice cold to room temperature, as long as it's not hot. Let the coffee bloom for a minute or so before giving it a stir to sink the grinds, then put the lid on (with the plunger still up) and allow it to sit for between 12 and 18 hours. When the brew time's finished, simply press the plunger down and pour the cold brew into another container for storage.

If you'd instead like to make your own home brewer, your first step is to assemble your supplies. You'll need an empty and clean two-liter bottle (with the lid), coffee filters (any shape will do), a piece of craft felt, a piece of thread, and a pair of scissors. Start by cutting the bottom off of the two-liter. Unscrew the cap, fold the piece of felt, and insert it firmly into the neck of the bottle, then screw the cap back on.

The next step is to prepare the coffee. Grind it coarse, then portion it out into 2-4 coffee filters (depending on their size). Don't overfill them; you want the grinds to have some space to move around inside. Tie each filter closed with a length of string to finish. Once these little packets are made, you can put them in your brewer. The only tricky thing about this method is that the bottle is bottomless and will need to stand cap-side down while the coffee brews. You'll need to find something sturdy to stand it up in while this happens—a Pyrex measuring cup or mason jar should do the trick, but since the coffee itself will never touch this vessel, you can use anything that will keep the bottle upright reliably.

Once you've found a stand for the bottle, add your water. Start by filling it about halfway, then move the coffee pouches around in the water, feeling them gently to work out any clumps or dry spots. If one of the filters tears during this point, it's not the end of the world; the felt is in the bottle to catch any stray grinds. Once all the coffee is thoroughly saturated, add the rest of your water, and let it brew for 12 to 24 hours. When you've finished the brew, remove the lid of the bottle, and allow the mix to drip through.

The obvious challenge with this method is that it's precarious and doesn't have a lid, so it's much more likely to be spilled. Instead of the bottle, you can use a sun tea jar or a beverage dispenser; any large vessel with a spigot at the bottom will do. You can find something of this nature at most home goods stores for around $15—certainly not as economical as a used pop bottle, but still less expensive than a cold brewing system.

Clean up and serving

If the grinds continue to make contact with the water longer than 24 hours, their structure will start to break down and they'll release particles and flavors into the brew you don't want to drink. Once you're satisfied with the brew level, drain the liquid into a separate, air-tight container for storage. Don't try to fish out the coffee packets from a DIY brewer. The time spent in the water weakens the filters, and they're likely to tear and leave you with a big mess on your hands. You can just dump them straight into the trash once you've removed the liquid. The bottle can be re-used for later brews, just wash it with soapy water after each. If you're using a French press, simply plunge, pour out the coffee, then dump the grinds and rinse the pot.

Because cold brew is concentrated compared to other brewing methods, you can control the strength of the cup you're drinking by how much additional liquid you add. For most people, a 1:1 ratio of cold water to cold brew concentrate is preferred, but you can adjust this to suit your own tastes. You can also add milk instead of water for a drink that tastes similar to an iced latte.

Other Brewing Methods

The brewing methods explored in the previous chapters cover the styles most people will encounter in their café or kitchen, but they are certainly not the only options out there. Coffee preparation has a long history, one which was influenced by a wide array of cultures. As you can see even from the many brewing methods already explored, this has resulted in an impressive variety of ways to turn this bean into a beverage.

The methods explored in this chapter are some you may or may not encounter in the course of your daily life but are worth noting nonetheless because of their uniqueness or historical popularity. They're included mostly just to introduce you to the wide array of possibilities when it comes to brewing coffee, but for the more adventurous java lover, they could be fun options to either seek out in a local specialty coffee shop or to try out in your own kitchen.

Coffee siphons

Also called a vacpot or a vacuum brewer, the coffee siphon looks like how a mad scientist would choose to brew his coffee. Made of glass and heated using a butane or alcohol burner (or, in some cases, over the stovetop), the siphon uses a combination of water pressure and immersion techniques to brew the coffee. It is one of the more theatrical ways to brew coffee, and many people who use one do so for the show of it; the downside is that the equipment can be costly, hard to come by, and delicate.

To brew in a coffee siphon, you want to start by putting the water in the lower globe of the assembly. You can start it cold, but it will take a long time to get up to temperature this way; many people prefer to boil the water first, then put it in. Put the filter and the top chamber on top of the bottom globe, making sure all the pieces are fit snugly into place. Grind the coffee using a fine setting (#6 or cone filter) with a similar ratio to what you'd use for immersion brewing. Place the ground coffee in the filter, then apply your heat source underneath the brewer.

As the water reaches boiling, the pressure of the steam will force it up through the coffee and into the upper chamber, where it will mingle with your grounds—a fun process to watch happen, that though it's based in science looks a lot like magic. Once the water starts to move into the upper chamber, start your timer. When it reaches 30 seconds, stir the coffee in a zig-zag pattern with a wooden paddle or spoon, until all the coffee grinds are submerged. When it reaches one minute, remove the heat source and stir the coffee again. As the water cools, it will automatically draw down through the grounds and back into the lower globe. This process should finish when the brew is around the two-minute mark.

Coffee brewed in a siphon will have a smooth and mellow flavor, with a relatively low acid content. It's especially good for bringing out subtle or delicate notes, especially those present in naturally-processed or high-grown varieties. They tend to use a cloth filter, as opposed to the paper or metal more common in other methods, the end result of which is a very clean cup without sediment. The combination of the cloth filter with the constant water temperature and the degree of control you get over the brewing time and agitation level means many coffee experts consider siphon brewing to be the ideal method.

Percolators

Interestingly, though percolators use a similar combination of air pressure and immersion to brew the coffee, the taste of the beverage they produce is almost universally panned by the coffee-drinking community. These devices, which are also known as Mokka pots or stovetop espresso makers, are stainless steel, hourglass-shaped brewers that sit directly on the burner of your stove as a heat source. The problem with them is that it's very difficult to gauge or maintain the water temperature, and they often end up boiling the coffee rather than brewing it, which can lead to a bitter cup of coffee with a faintly metallic taste that's overly strong and thick.

Percolators were a popular brewing method in the first half of the twentieth century. At that time, they produced a cup that was superior in taste to the technique most people used previously, which was simply to put the ground coffee in a pot with boiling water. Percolators do produce a strong coffee aroma, but this, unfortunately, is the result of most of the volatile compounds cooking off, meaning you won't get those tastes in the cup you're drinking.

While you'll find some people who prefer the taste of percolator coffee, it's usually out of habit and familiarity more than anything; if they grew up drinking that thick, bitter brew, that's what they're looking for in their cup. For modern drinkers, however, it's best to steer clear. You can brew much better coffee much more easily with most other methods.

Turkish coffee

This method of brewing may have been one of the earliest—if not the earliest—technique applied to make a beverage out of coffee beans. It is one of the simplest brewing methods you'll find. Simply grind the coffee and place it in a pot with some water and sugar, then bring it to a boil three times. It's typically served immediately after brewing in small, handle-less cups.

Unlike most brewing methods, Turkish coffee is not filtered before serving. It is also ground very fine, even finer than espresso; if you have a burr grinder, you'll see that the "Turkish" setting is the finest option on your machine. Most of the grinds will sink to the bottom of the cup while you're drinking, but you should expect to get some in your mouth while you're drinking. There is a tradition of reading your fortune or future in the pattern of the grounds left behind after you drink the beverage, similarly to how tea leaves are read in some places.

The taste of Turkish coffee is distinctive. It is very strong and very thick, with a touch of sweetness from the sugar in the brew. Compared to familiar brewing methods, it will be similar to espresso but with even more body and a grittiness from the included grinds. It's an acquired taste for most Western palates, but can be a fun method to play around with since it can be made without any extra equipment.

It's Up to You

Even as recently as the early 1990s, coffee was brewed very differently in the United States than it is in the modern day. There was a habit of using too low of a coffee to water ratio. This would often result in a thin and weak cup of coffee, likely part of the reason why the tastes at that time were skewed more toward very dark roasts, whose heavy flavors would come out even in a weak brew. The specialty coffee movement changed this practice, but there is still some disagreement between generations about just what a good cup of coffee means.

Coffee should be a sensory experience. The aroma is inextricably linked to the taste, and the feel of the drink on your tongue is just as important as the subtle notes that you bring out in the brew. Most of the brewing practices outlined in the preceding chapters are aimed at preserving the volatile oils that give coffee its distinctive smell and making sure that all of the right compounds are extracted—the principle of take the best, leave the rest.

The wide array of options you have for brewing methods in the modern era of specialty and single-origin coffees can be overwhelming if you're not a student of the bean. Choosing which one is right for you can be a challenge, especially if you haven't had direct contact or experience with anything save espresso and drip.

If you're on a tight budget and want to get the best flavor for your money, you'll find Aeropress, French press, and pour over to be the most affordable, both in terms of the initial investment and the economy of coffee used in them. If you're more concerned about convenience and the amount of time it takes you to make your daily cup, a high-end drip machine with automated features can brew your coffee before you even get up in the morning. Immersion brewers take a bit longer but can be equally convenient since you can walk away while your beverage steeps.

If you travel a lot, you probably want a reliable way to brew good coffee that you can take with you. The Aeropress is an excellent choice for this because it's compact and durable. Clever and plastic pour-over brewers are also great choices for portability. These same recommendations apply if you have limited kitchen space to work with and want to buy the most compact brewing option available.

Barring these kinds of considerations, the right brewing method is all about the taste. If you like drinking more delicate light roasts, go for a pour over, a Chemex, or a siphon; they'll be the most likely to bring out brighter notes without muddling them. If you prefer a stronger cup or a darker roast, an immersion brewer will be more your speed; espresso also works quite well with dark roasts. If you have a sensitive stomach and want to get the lowest acidity, a cold brew method is your answer.

The truth is, the right brew method is whichever one you feel gives you the most enjoyable drinking experience. Experimenting with different methods as much as your budget and living space allow is the best way to decide which one you like the best. Understanding what makes each brewing method result in the flavors it does will help to guide your decision, but as was mentioned in the introduction, practice and experience will be your best teachers.

Tasting Coffee

Coffee Cupping Techniques to Unleash the Bean!

JESSICA SIMSS

The Idea Behind Coffee Tasting

There is both an art and a science to tasting coffee. The overall flavor profile of coffee is assertive and distinctive; if you've never tried to identify the specific notes, you may just think that every cup you drink simply tastes like coffee, especially if you typically add milk and sugar to your beverages. The truth is, though, that there are a lot of subtle variations and flavor differences between different cultivars and varieties, as well as between coffees that have been grown, processed, or roasted differently. Being able to identify these differences can open up a whole new world of coffee for you to enjoy.

When people talk about the flavor notes of coffee, this doesn't mean that the coffees themselves have been flavored. Rather, this is referring to the other flavors that are developed within the bean and add complexity to the overall flavor profile. Picking these notes out from each other can be tricky, especially for the novice taster, requiring both practice and attention to identify. The good news is you don't need to be a barista to taste these subtle notes. A well-trained palate can be developed over time, even if you have no professional experience in coffee.

The idea behind a coffee tasting is to isolate the specific characteristics of a single variety. While you can do a tasting with blends, you'll get more value out of tasting single-origin coffees, since this will allow you to more clearly identify the specific taste characteristics in that bean. It's important to maintain uniformity throughout and across the samples, as well, to avoid adding any extra flavor variations into the mix, like those caused by different roast levels, grind levels, and brew methods.

Even between exceptional coffees, not all of them will taste the same. The goal with coffee is not to produce beans of identical quality but to bring out the maximum potential of each bean—in other words, having it be the best version of itself. Some coffees will have more sweetness, and some more acidity; some will be velvety in the texture, while others will be thinner in your mouth. Part of the purpose of a tasting is to identify which qualities of coffee are most appealing to you and finding the beans that exhibit all of those characteristics.

Tasting coffee first means understanding the flavors it contains and how to identify them yourself. Both sides of this are explored in the chapters that follow in this book. Just like with wine, there is a community and tradition built around tasting coffee, and industry professionals have designed flavor wheels that identify some of the key flavor notes and other attributes found in many coffees. Studying and understanding these will be a great benefit in setting up your own tasting, but will be useless if you haven't developed your palate to be able to detect subtleties of flavor. Knowledge and skill must be built up together for a truly successful tasting.

Supplies for Home Tasting

For the most part, the supplies you need for setting up a coffee tasting at home are the same ones you'll use for general brewing, but there are some specialized pieces of equipment that will be helpful to have on hand. If you want to get the professional tasters' version of this equipment, you can buy it online from the Specialty Coffee Association of America (SCAA, for short), but you can also use things that you have around your own home or buy less expensive versions of the same basic tools from your local kitchen supply or department store.

The idea behind a coffee tasting is to get as true a sense as possible of what notes and flavor characteristics the bean exhibits. This means you'll want to limit as many variables as possible that could change the consistency of your brew or alter the flavor of the bean. It's imperative that you grind the beans at home, immediately before brewing, to avoid the loss of volatile compounds that contribute to the coffee's flavor and aroma. Similarly, you'll want to weigh the beans and use a specific quantity of water, even if you're typically in the habit of eyeballing these amounts, so you can be sure differences in flavor are due to differences in the bean and not variations in the brewing method.

Because of this, the kinds of supplies you'll need to actually purchase before setting up your own home coffee tasting will vary greatly depending on how sophisticated your current brewing set-up is. If you already have a burr grinder and a gram scale, for example, your purchases will be minimal; if you typically use pre-ground coffee, on the other hand, you'll need to spend a bit of extra money to get the right equipment before attempting a tasting.

The sections that follow in this chapter will walk you through every piece of equipment required for a tasting, why you need it, and what kind you should buy. Coffee tasting is a time-sensitive process. The taste and aroma of coffee can change significantly as it brews and then cools. Achieving perfect consistency in all the samples means being able to grind, brew, and taste all of your samples on the same basic schedule. Because of this, you'll probably find it best to not only purchase all of your supplies before starting, but also to assemble them in one place for easy access before you pour your first beans into the grinder.

Cups

There are two sets of cups that you'll need for setting up your own home cupping lab: the containers for holding the portioned-out beans in preparation for brewing, and the glasses you'll be brewing into. The containers that you portion the beans into don't have to follow any specific guidelines, so long as they'll hold enough beans for a single brew. Small bowls, Tupperware containers, or disposable plastic or paper cups will function nicely for your purposes. You could even use extra coffee filters or cupcake wrappers in a pinch.

The brewing cups need to follow slightly more stringent guidelines. They should have a capacity of around 5-7 ounces, and should be approximately the same size. You should also pick a cup made of a material with a relatively good heat retention. Ceramic and glass are ideal. Rocks glasses (like those used for many mixed drinks) tend to be a good option, but you can also use dishes or bowls, provided they have the right volume. Whatever kind of vessel you brew in, you should make sure that it has a relatively wide mouth, at least wide enough for two spoons at once so that you can properly skim the grinds off of the top during the process.

How many bean containers and brewing glasses you need will depend on how many samples you want to test at one time. If you're tasting with a group of four or more, you will likely want to have two cups for each type of coffee you're testing so that everyone will get the same opportunity to taste and smell the brewed beverage. Many professional tasters will brew three versions of each sample as a matter, of course, to account for potential inconsistencies in the roast or bean and make sure they're getting a thorough profile of the coffee in question. As a home taster, you can choose whether or not you want to follow this same pattern; it may be a factor of how many cups you have available to use.

Spoons

Like with the cups, professional tasters use specialized spoons for sampling. These are shallower and wider than the average spoon from your silverware drawer and are also typically silver-plated. This is more than simply aesthetics; spoons made of steel, plastic, or other materials can subtly alter the taste of the coffee that you're sampling.

For home tasting, you don't necessarily need to worry about the material that's been used in making your spoon, although metal is generally better than plastic. The main thing you should pay attention to is the size and shape of the spoon. You want something that's shallower and wider than the typical spoon you'd use to eat your cereal in the morning. If you can find soup spoons, these will work better than standard spoons for tasting purposes.

You won't need quite as many spoons as you do cups for your tasting because you won't need a designated spoon for each sample, provided you keep a cup of clean water on the tasting table to rinse the spoon between coffees. A set of four total spoons should be sufficient, regardless of how many coffees you're tasting.

Scale

Different coffee beans will have different densities depending on their growing conditions and roast level. Because of this, weight is a much more accurate way to measure coffee than volume, and since accuracy and consistency are paramount in coffee tasting, you'll need to have a scale to do it effectively.

A digital scale with gram measurements is going to be your best bet. Dial scales simply will not give you the degree of accuracy and precision you'll want for a truly successful tasting. Look for one that can measure with a precision of at least .1 grams (.01 grams is even better). If you don't already have one, you can buy a fairly reliable and effective one for around $30 from most kitchen supply and department stores.

Grinder

Likely the most expensive piece of equipment you'll need to buy if you don't have one already is a quality burr grinder. Blade coffee grinders are inexpensive, but they can't give you the grind consistency you need either between or within batches to really get a sense of the different flavors. This is because the fineness of the grind in a blade grinder is based on how long it runs, leading to a large variation between the different pieces that result, and making it much harder to get the grind to the same level every time. With a burr grinder, the coffee beans crushed between metal plates, with the distance between them determining the grind size, allowing for far more control.

There are different styles of burr grinders. Generally speaking, the more expensive the model, the more fine-tuning it allows on the part of the brewer. Because you'll be using an immersion method to brew for a tasting, you don't need to worry about getting a high-end espresso grinder. You can find a reliable burr grinder for around $100 to $200. While this might seem like a hefty investment, it will also improve the quality of your coffee drinking experience, regardless of your brewing method.

Kettle and water

You will need to have some way to heat your water for your brew. It's not recommended to heat up your water in the microwave or in a saucepan on the stovetop; this can give it a flat taste that affects the flavor of the cup. Either an electric or a stovetop kettle should suit your needs nicely. While gooseneck kettles can be helpful in controlling the amount of water that comes out at any given time, they're not strictly necessary for coffee tasting the way they are for manual brewing methods like pour over and Chemex. More important than the way the water pours is that you are able to pour the same amount consistently in each tasting cup.

When it comes to what kind of water you use, this will likely be a factor of the area where you live. If the water that comes out of your tap has a relatively low mineral content, you should have no problem using it to brew your tasting samples. If the water is especially hard, contains high amounts of chemicals like chlorine, or if there is a lime scale problem in your region, you may want to consider bottled options. Most brewers recommend avoiding distilled water, as this can make your coffee taste flat, in a similar way to heating the water in a microwave. Whether you use filtered water, natural spring water, or reverse osmosis water is up to you. Again, the main thing that's important is consistency across tastings.

Coffee

Obviously, the most important aspect of any coffee tasting is the coffee itself. You'll want to have a range of coffees to compare to each other. You should use at least three different varieties to give you an adequate range of flavors. Each tasting portion will use around 12 grams of coffee. A quarter pound of each variety you're tasting should be more than enough for two tasting portions and a bit left over in case you make a mistake along the way.

You can use any coffee that you want to for a coffee tasting, but you should consider the roast level before you buy. Dark roasts will obscure some of the original flavors of the bean; a light or medium roast will reveal more of the true nature of the coffee. If the surface of the coffee bean is shiny, it's probably roasted too dark to use in this context. When you're first starting out, you'll find it more valuable to choose beans with a wide range of flavor profiles. It will be easier to taste the differences between an Ethiopia and a Sumatra, for example, than to pick out a Guatemala from a Costa Rica. As you gain more experience, you can narrow your selections, tasting coffees grow in more closely related regions—or even different processing methods or farms within the same region—to note the subtle changes.

Tasting journal

When professional coffee tasters cup their beans, they have forms that they fill out, with designated spaces to grade and evaluate various aspects of the drinking experience. You certainly don't need to go to this extreme with your home tastings, but keeping a journal or a book of notes is likely to be beneficial. By recording what you taste in various coffees when you cup them, you can hone in on which beans produce flavors that you like. This will help you establish a frame of reference for your future tastings, honing and developing your palate.

The Taster's Vocabulary

It's one thing to be able to taste the different notes and textures that a certain bean produces, but this won't be very helpful if you don't have the language to express it. If you have some experience with wine tasting, many of these terms will be familiar to you, but coffee does have its own set of terminology and common flavor characteristics that even experienced sommeliers will have to learn.

When it comes to the flavor notes themselves, it's more about being able to pick out specific tastes than it is learning words. Where a lot of the confusion over coffee tasting comes into play is with the overarching flavor descriptors and the terms that describe various aspects of the mouthfeel or texture. The sections that follow in this chapter will give you a brief introduction to these categorical terms, what the specific designations mean, and the impact they have on the flavor of your final cup.

Taste versus aromatics

The flavor of a coffee is a combination of two distinct categories of compounds: aromatics and tastes. Aromatic compounds are extremely volatile. They begin to dissipate into the atmosphere as soon as you grind the coffee, and once they've evaporated into the atmosphere they cannot be recovered. This means they're also readily extracted by hot water and are often the first things to dissolve into the cup of coffee. In terms of the overall weight of the coffee bean, they comprise only a negligible amount, but they have a huge impact on your perception of the coffee's taste. The continued evaporation of aromatic compounds over time is one of the reasons that coffee changes flavor so dramatically as it cools, and is also why it's generally best to enjoy your coffee immediately after preparation.

Taste compounds, on the other hand, extract more slowly. These come from water-soluble, non-volatile compounds like caffeine, carbohydrates, and trigonelline. They do not dissipate after the coffee is ground; in fact, the longer you brew the coffee, the more of these compounds will be extracted.

In terms of over-arching tastes, the standard flavor categories apply. The ideal cup of coffee strikes a balance between tastes that are sweet, sour, salty, savory, and bitter; some of the most lauded and complex coffee has definite notes from all five of these categories. Generally speaking, however, the flavor of most concern to coffee drinkers is the sweetness. This is the aspect that is considered by many to separate good coffee from great coffee, as it provides an excellent balance to the coffee's natural bitterness and acidity. You'll find that many of the sweet and sour notes come from the aromatics, while the bitter, salty, and savory notes are from the taste compounds, but this is far from a hard and fast rule.

Acidity

Also described as "brightness" or "sharpness," the acidity of a coffee is different than the sour notes you'll get from the flavor characteristics. Acidity often goes hand in hand with fruit and floral notes, but it is also a texture descriptor, describing the way the coffee feels on your tongue, often on the front edge of the taste. Acidity is one of the most scrutinized characteristics of coffee, in part because a good acidity level is seen as the hallmark of a successful cup of coffee.

If you're having trouble visualizing how acidity is different from a sour flavor, consider the taste sensation of biting into a green apple, or sucking on a lemon wedge. There is a certain physical sensation that accompanies this, a kind of "sparkle" on your tongue, that's different from the flavors the fruit brings.

When talking about the brightness of a coffee, certain descriptors are commonly used. For the degree of acidity, you can use terms like "intense" or "mild." There are also different qualities to the acidity. It can be sharp, edgy, rough, or rounded, or some variation of those, in addition to the varying intensity. It's easiest to evaluate the acidity once the coffee has had a chance to cool slightly, so you may notice it more on your second or third pass. Acidity tends to be enhanced by pressurized brews, like espresso.

Body

You may also hear this referred to as the coffee's "mouthfeel." It can be roughly defined as the weight of the coffee in your mouth. You can also think of it as the coffee's viscosity or thickness, and describes how much presence the coffee seems to have when you're holding it in your mouth. "Body can sometimes be tricky for beginners to identify. If you're having trouble pinpointing descriptors for the coffee's body, try moving it around your mouth for a bit longer before swallowing.

The body of a coffee comes mostly from the insoluble materials that are in it, like the lipids, fats, or fine coffee particulates. These bind together within the cup to form colloids. While these compounds increase the body, they can also muddy the flavor if they're too plentiful within the brew.

Body is one of the characteristics most affected by the brewing method that you use. Different brewing methods will allow different amounts of insoluble material into the cup. Espresso tends to have the most body, both because the coffee to water ratio is relatively high and because the perforated metal of the portafilter allows more dissolved solids through into the brew. Methods that use a paper filter, like Chemex or pour over, will have a lighter body since more of the solids are filtered out. Immersion brewing methods will be somewhere in the middle, one of the reasons why it is a popular method for tastings.

There are many different terms you can use to describe the body of a coffee. If it has a relatively light body, you might use terms like watery, slick, juicy, silky, or tea-like. A medium body will be more like 2% milk—smooth and creamy, sometimes with a syrupy or round characteristic. A heavy body might be described using words like full, velvety, or even chewy. The fuller the body, the more you'll feel it coating the inside of your mouth after you drink.

Finish

The lingering effect of the coffee after you've swallowed it, both in regards to its taste and its texture, is referred to as the finish. You may also hear this called the coffee's aftertaste. This is an important part of the coffee drinking experience. A good coffee should linger for a little while after you've swallowed, though the notes that linger are equally important to determine its overall quality.

The ideal coffee has a sweet, clean finish, with a taste that stays on your tongue for around 10-15 seconds after swallowing. It should reinforce the best notes of the coffee, without feeling too rough or bitter, and should have a similar complexity to the initial taste. There is often a direct correlation between the body and the finish, with a fuller body typically granting a more lingering aftertaste, though there are certainly exceptions to this rule. Similar to the body, the finish will be affected by the brewing method. Espresso tends to have the most aftertaste because of the many oils and trapped gasses contained in both the liquor and the crema.

Flavor Wheels

The first flavor wheel specifically for coffee was designed by the SCAA in the 1980s. This flavor wheel remained unchanged for over two decades. Its 2016 revision was concurrent with the expansion of the lexicon, a book which established the specific and definable taste that could be associated with each of the 110 contained attributes, giving each one a reference product that is both brand specific and widely available. This revision project was one of the most extensive collaborative research projects ever undertaken for the coffee industry and established a new set of vocabulary for use by professionals and amateurs alike.

The coffee lexicon is a separate document that exists independently of the flavor wheel, though the flavors defined in it form the foundation of the tastes listed on the wheel. It is an invaluable tool for professional cuppers, for the first time giving the industry a standardized language to use when they're discussing coffee notes. It was built by the organization World Coffee Research, in conjunction with a research group based out of Kansas State University, and is an invaluable tool for coffee professionals. For amateur tasters, however, the flavor wheel itself should be plenty comprehensive on its own.

Since the creation of the first SCAA flavor wheel, other companies in the coffee industry have designed their own versions of the model. These are often very similar to the official SCAA version but have variations designed to better-suit the specific coffees utilized by the company. The majority of these were developed well before the 2016 revision that standardized the lexicon; it is yet to be seen how the existence of the new SCAA flavor wheel will affect the use of these alternate versions.

The sections that follow in this chapter will explore in depth two different flavor wheels that you may find particularly useful. The first is the revised SCAA wheel; the second, the wheel designed by Counter Culture, an independent roaster that provides coffee to artesian cafes throughout the United States. If you would like to see a visual representation of these coffee wheels, they're widely available for free online; simply type the name of the coffee wheel you want to see into your chosen search engine. You may find it helpful to print a copy of your preferred wheel and keep it on the table during your tasting for quick and easy reference.

The SCAA flavor wheel

The very center of the SCAA flavor wheel is broken into two halves: tastes and aromas. Each of these is then divided into sub-categories that extend outwards, getting more specific as they go. The "tastes" half of the wheel is where you'll find a lot of descriptors that have to do with the feel and body of the coffee; the "aromas" half is the domain of more familiar flavor names, associated with common foods and ingredients.

The tastes side of the wheel is further divided into four broad sections: sour, sweet, salt, and bitter, the four main established zones of the tongue, though excluding the more recently added "savory" or "umami" region. Each of these is then divided into smaller units which give you an array of potential words that you can use to describe the coffee's taste. Within sour, you'll find terms like acrid, hard, tart, and tangy. Sweet is divided between acidic sweetness (piquant or nippy) and mellow sweetness, with suggested terms of mild or delicate. With salt, the division is between bland and sharp flavors. Finally, the bitter category is divided into harsh terms, like alkaline or caustic, and pungent terms, indicating phenolic or creosol flavors.

The aromas side of the wheel is also sub-divided initially into three sections: enzymatic, sugar browning, and dry distillation. This half is the inverse of the tastes half, in the sense that the descriptors will likely become more familiar to you as you move further out. Within the enzymatic category are flavors that are fruity (citrus or berry-like flavor), flowery (floral and fragrant flavors), and herby (whether alliaceous, like onion and garlic, or leguminous, like peas or cucumbers). The sugar browning section is divided into categories for nut, caramel, or chocolate flavors. Finally, the dry distillation section is where you'll find flavors that are carbony, spicy, or resinous. This last category contains some flavors that might not seem desirable at first blush, like the medicinal category of the resinous section, or the burnt, charred, and tarry descriptors you'll find in the carbony section.

The Counter Culture flavor wheel

There is no central half and half division in the Counter Culture flavor wheel. Instead, it looks much more similar to the tasting wheel that's used by sommeliers to taste wine. It is divided into ten broad sections, each of which represents a different category of flavors which are commonly found in coffee, color-coded to make it easier to navigate.

The most detailed section of the wheel is the "fruit" section. This makes sense, given the prominence of fruit flavors in most coffees. The section is further divided into eight smaller categories, each of which has its own associated specific fruit tastes. These include citrus, apple/pear, melon, grape (which also includes wine), tropical fruit, stone fruit (fruits with pits, like cherry, plum, apricot, and peach), berry, and dried fruit.

The other nine sections of the wheel have only one further layer of division, into specific flavors associated with that group. Working counterclockwise, the next grouping is "floral." The floral category is comprised mostly of aromatics as opposed to tastes and includes such flavors as hibiscus, lavender, jasmine, orange blossom, and lemongrass. There is often a fine division between these flavors and those included in the next category, labeled "vegetal, earthy, herb." This includes herbs common from most kitchens, like dill, mint, and sage, as well as vegetable flavors sometimes found in coffee, such as peas, green pepper, olive, squash, and leafy greens. This is also where you'll find tastes associated with other growing things. Positive fungal or earthy, soil flavors will be found under this category. If there are notes of cedar, wood, hay, or tobacco, these will be included in this category, as will tastes more commonly associated with other beverages, like hops, bergamot, black tea, green tea, or grassiness.

The "savory" category is relatively small and includes anything that will give you the umami notes associated more often with food. The most commonly encountered entry in this category is a tomato note, especially when it comes to the acidity; you may also taste notes of soy sauce, meatiness, or leather. This is differentiated from the "spice" category that follows to the left, which includes flavors like licorice, nutmeg, ginger, cinnamon, coriander, and pepper.

The next category to the left is where you'll find the notes imparted by the roasting, including subcategories of carbon, smoke, burnt sugar, or toast. After that is a section for grain or cereal notes, things like fresh bread, graham crackers, granola, or pastries, along with raw grains like barley, wheat, and rye.

The three categories along the bottom of the flavor wheel are those that you will likely get the most notes from as you taste, with flavors that tend to be even more prominent than the fruity and floral notes so prized in high-quality coffees. The "nut" and "chocolate" categories are fairly self-explanatory, but you may need to study the entries under "sweet and sugary." Tastes featured here include sugar variants like brown sugar, sugar cane, honey, and molasses, as well as syrupy and sugary flavors in general, like cola, caramel, maple syrup, and marshmallows. Flavors generally associated with baking are also included in this category, with such options as butter, cream, nougat, and vanilla.

The Counter Culture flavor wheel, in general, is designed to be easily used by a taster who's only interested in the actual notes and flavors that hit their tongue and is less concerned with the compound that contributes the flavors, making no distinction between tastes and aromas. It also sticks to flavors that can be considered desirable. This doesn't necessarily mean that every coffee drinker is looking for cedar or smoke notes (for example), but that there are situations in which every note listed on this flavor wheel can come from a well-roasted, well-brewed, high-quality coffee. Counter Culture has a separate flavor wheel for off tastes (explored in more depth in chapter 5), which is different from the SCAA flavor wheel, which incorporates both desirable and undesirable flavors. This can make the Counter Culture wheel a bit more intuitive for non-professionals, helping to differentiate the flavors you want from the ones you don't.

Using Flavor Wheels

Whichever flavor wheel you choose to use as a reference, the array of options can be a bit overwhelming to someone who hasn't spent a lot of time training their palate. This is especially true of the SCAA flavor wheel, which includes both familiar descriptors and more conceptual terms, like clean, vibrant, and sturdy—words that you may not have a point of reference in your mind for associating with a taste.

The flavor wheel is intended as an aid to tasting, not a detriment. It is not intended to be prescriptive. If you taste something in the coffee that isn't on the wheel, that doesn't mean you're wrong; coffee is constantly evolving, with new varietals, processing methods, and roasting practices bringing new tastes into the mix that may not have been prevalent before. This is further complicated by the fact that everyone's palate is unique. Two people drinking the same cup of coffee might pick out completely different flavors from it.

You also don't necessarily need to use food-based terminology to describe the flavors in the coffee. Smell and taste are two senses very heavily associated with memories and your own background and experiences. You can use words like "summery" or "wild" if the flavors in a given cup seem to align with those terms in your mind. Other non-food descriptors that are common include words like bright, crisp, dull, pointed, balanced, deep, delicate, dirty, juicy, or complex. You can also use modifiers freely, pairing terms like faint, lingering, muted, or strong with other terms to get a more specific and accurate picture of what your tongue is getting out of the coffee. The end goal is to give a purposeful description of the coffee that can communicate its essence in a way that other people can relate to, and a way that you'll be able to interpret and understand when you go back and look at your notes later.

When you're using a flavor wheel, you want to work from the inside out. Start by figuring out which general category the taste will fall into—whether it's floral or fruity, for example, or more nutty or chocolatey. From there, you can start to get more specific, working outward until you've identified the exact flavor. You may not be able to achieve this degree of specificity when you're first tasting. It could be that you can tell there's a fruity element, or even that it's some form of citrus, but won't be able to discern whether it reminds you more of orange or lemon. This is fine, especially for a beginner. Whatever notes you can make, even if they're vague, will help you to better understand the coffee and its flavors.

Also, keep in mind that good coffee won't only have one note. It should be a very complex combination of flavors from various points of the flavor wheel. You may taste the acidity of a lemon along with the sweetness of brown sugar and hints of raspberry or almond all at the same time. Picking these flavors apart from each other can be one of the trickiest aspects of tasting coffee, especially for a lay person. This is why it's often helpful to taste in groups. You may be able to identify the nuttiness, while your friend might have a better perception of the brighter, citrus tones. By working together, you can construct the full profile of the flavor, helping each other to identify the many various notes contained in a given bean.

The flavor of coffee is too complex to really generalize, with too many factors affecting the taste at each step of the bean's lifespan. Having said that, however, one of the best ways for a beginning taster to wrap their minds around the world of tasting is to attach certain notes or flavors with the general profiles of beans from certain geographical areas. These rules are certainly not set in stone, and you'll find a lot of variation between beans from the same region even before accounting for such factors as the roast level or the brewing practices. Constructing a general flavor profile for a certain region's coffee can be helpful, however, letting you get a sense of what to look out for and expect from a given cup—so long as you're prepared for the fact that there will be anomalies and flavors that don't align with what the coffee from a given region is "supposed to" taste like.

Central American regional profiles

Coffees from Central America are often some of the easiest for a beginning taster to work with. They are almost entirely wet processed and grow in a fairly similar climate across countries, which tend to use more standardized growing practices. This combination of factors can give them a more consistent taste profile with fewer surprises or variations.

General terms used to describe Central American coffees include bright, clean, and balanced. They will tend to have a mix of smooth, brown sugar or caramel sweetness with a more tart fruit-like acidity. The texture can be smooth like rich chocolate or more buttery, like a pastry crust, but the body does tend more toward the medium or thin side. Costa Rican coffees are often especially light and refreshing with strong citrus notes, often grapefruit or lemon flavors. Coffees from Guatemala tend to have a more apple or pear-like fruitiness and acidity, while those from Honduras and Nicaragua tend to give you more of a tropical fruit flavor, with notes of mango or pineapple.

You can also include coffees from North America and the Caribbean in the Central American category, as they will often share a similar flavor profile. This includes coffees from Hawaii, which are more American in nature despite the fact that the islands are closer geographically to Southeast Asia. Coffee from Kona is especially known for having an apricot finish. If you're buying a coffee from Jamaica, expect a similar clean taste profile to what you'd get from a Central American coffee, though with a slightly creamier body and more floral than fruity notes.

Coffee from Mexico shows the most variation of any from this category, owing mainly to the differing climate conditions between the regions of the country. Coffee from the Oaxaca region will have the lightest body and acidity, while that from the Chiapas region tends to have strong notes of nut and caramel and a thicker body, more similar to coffees from Guatemala. If there are fruity notes, it tends to be a cherry-like acidity or other flavors from the stone fruit category.

South American regional profiles

While there are certainly many similarities between the coffees grown in Central America and the ones from South America—owing largely to the use of similar varieties, growing practices, and processing methods—but the greater degree of variation in the climate conditions and elevations in turn means there is more variation in the flavor profiles, as well.

Coffees from Colombia tend to be sweeter and less acidic. Though they can be bright with mild fruity notes, you're more likely to taste notes of nut, chocolate, caramel, or maple syrup. You can expect a smooth texture with a medium body from most Colombian varieties. Coffees from the Nariño region will have a slightly higher acidity, owing to the volcanic soil typically used for growing.

The other major coffee-producing nation in South America is Brazil. These beans are grown generally at a low altitude than most others from the region, which results in a cup that's less clean, with a lower acidity and fewer fruit or floral notes. You can expect a relatively heavy body, which may be syrupy or may be creamier, with a lingering aftertaste. If you're looking for flavor notes, expect to find them in the nut and chocolate portion of the flavor wheel, potentially with grain-like or malty undertones.

African regional profiles

Complexity is the main buzz word when it comes to African coffees. If you want to taste a coffee that will give you a wide array of notes from all quadrants of the flavor wheel, African beans are a good way to go. You can find coffees from this region that are processed using both wet and dry methods; each of these will give you a slightly different set of flavor profiles, even within beans grown in the same country (or even on the same farm). This is also the only country that produces wild-grown coffee along with cultivated or farm-grown trees, introducing a degree of wildness and unpredictability into the crops from this continent. Regardless of which country the coffee is from, you can expect African coffees to be fragrant, strong, and full-bodied, with significant fruit and floral notes.

Ethiopian coffees come predominantly from three regions: Harrar, Sidamo, and Yirgacheffe. If they're wet-processed, they will have a thinner, more tea-like texture that's drier on the palate, with a shorter aftertaste. The notes in a wet-processed Ethiopian are more delicate and often from the floral quadrant of the flavor wheel; look for tastes like jasmine, hibiscus, and lemongrass. Dry-processed or natural Ethiopians, on the other hand, tend to be syrupy or juicy in their body and are known for bright fruit flavors. Look for berry notes, like strawberry and blueberry, when you're tasting a natural Ethiopian.

Coffees from Kenya are known for being bold and juicy, both in flavor and mouthfeel. The acidity is prominent but may be more savory than sweet, varying between a tomato-like acidity and a tart, mouth-puckering punch that's more like black currant. The sweetness generally comes from the fruity side of the spectrum. Depending on the region, you may find tropical notes like mango and papaya, citrus notes like orange and grapefruit, or berry notes like raspberry and blueberry.

These are the two main exporters of coffee from Africa, but you can also find beans grown in a whole host of other countries. Coffees from Tanzania are popular in part because the nation's crops produce a lot of peaberries, a genetic mutation of the beans that makes them rounder and denser than typical coffee beans. This gives them a bright, citrus acidity, with a juicy body and floral and fruit notes ranging from jasmine to black currant. Coffees from Rwanda, meanwhile, tend to have an acidity more like green apple, bright and punch, with fresh floral notes. Coffee from Burundi is more similar to Kenyans, clean in flavor with berry notes in both the taste and the aroma and a thick, rich body.

Coffees grown in the Middle East tend to have a similar flavor profile to coffees from Africa and can be considered in the same category for practical purposes. The most prominent growing region of the Middle East is Yemen. You can expect a full-bodied coffee from this region, often with an acidity that's winey rather than fruit-like. There is often a musky, spicy note to the flavor—look for dry fruit notes along with cinnamon, cardamom, tobacco, or chocolate.

Asian regional profiles

There is nearly as much variation between coffees grown in Asian nations as there is with those grown in Africa, and for many of the same reasons: regional variations in growing and processing methods. More so than with any other region, Asian coffees tend to have the assertive, unique flavors that make them a "love or hate" kind of coffee.

This is especially true of the many varieties from Indonesia. In general, these coffees will be dark and earthy, with more savory notes and lower acidity. There are often spicy flavor notes, and the body is typically on the heavier side, especially when the beans have been dry-processed. Because Indonesia is an island of nations, the variations between islands will be as marked as the variations between countries in other regions. Coffees from Java tend to be the mildest of the Indonesian coffees, giving you the cleanest cup, especially when they're wet-processed; look for nutty, malty, and chocolatey notes with a bright acidity and a relatively light body. Conversely, coffees from Sumatra tend to be the most complex and unique. You'll likely taste flavors from the savory and herby portions of the wheel, with a rich earthiness that can be mushroom-like or stout-like. Depending on the variety and the roast, however, you may also taste spicy notes (especially anise and clove) or smoky, roasted flavors, with woody or chocolatey undertones.

Another Pacific island nation known for its coffee production is Papua New Guinea. Most of the coffee crops here grow in volcanic soil, which gives them a bright, clean acidity, pronounced sweetness, and syrupy, full body. You may taste some of the earthiness found in Indonesian coffees, but it more often ends up on the sour, bright side of the wheel, with notes of tart fruits like currant, lemon, and cherry.

You may occasionally also see coffee grown in India. The majority of these beans come from the state of Karnataka, which is often labeled as Mysore (the former name of the state). It is usually wet processed, meaning it has a cleaner cup and thinner body than the coffees of Indonesia, for example, though it still tends to exhibit a similar complexity, combining bright and sweet fruity notes with darker spice and roasted flavors.

There is also a particular processing method, called Monsooning, which is only widely practiced in Asian coffee production. This involves allowing the picked coffee cherries to be exposed to the moist air of the monsoon season for a little while, "aging" the coffee beans and letting them ferment before they're sent through the rest of the process. A monsooned coffee bean will be paler, and the flavor tends to be a milder, creamy, smoother version of the un-monsooned version of the bean. Monsooning increases the body and reduces the acidity; it may also take on a slightly fermented flavor, similar to wine or brandy. This is typically seen most with Indian coffees, though you may also find Indonesian monsooned varieties.

Identifying Off Flavors

Most of the flavors on the flavor wheel aren't inherently good or bad. Some notes are less universally admired than others—especially on the savory and earthy sides of the wheel—but whether they're considered "good" or not is a matter of personal preference. Perhaps more importantly, their presence in the cup is not a symptom of a problem with the bean at some stage of its growth or production. Those are tastes that are naturally occurring, however rare or controversial they may be.

There are other flavors, though, that should be seen as an indication of a deeper ill. Being able to identify a good acidity from the sourness of an improper brew, or telling the difference between a coffee that's moldy and one that simply has earthy notes, is one of the main skills a professional coffee taster has to develop.

The good news for a home taster is that the beans you're buying have most likely already been vetted for quality. You're not deciding which green coffee beans you're going to be purchasing lots of for your roasting purposes; the roaster you're buying from has people who have already seen to that. Still, being able to identify the probable source of off flavors can help you gain a better understanding of the coffee that you drink.

As was mentioned in chapter 3, Counter Culture has a flavor wheel of only off flavors commonly found in coffee beans, conveniently divided by the probable source of the imperfection or issue. You can find a version of this wheel online for free as well if you'd rather have a visual aid for your tasting. It is used just like other coffee wheels, with broader categories in the center of the wheel that branch out to more specific tastes as you go outward. The center-most circle is divided into seven categories: mold, aged or faded, tainted, over-roasted, under-roasted, under-ripe, and fruit decomposition.

A coffee also doesn't have to have any one specific "bad" taste to be a lower-quality coffee. Complexity and balance are two characteristics that many professional coffee tasters look for in their beans. If a bean is said to be flat or to lack character, this is a way of saying the taste experience is too one-note. This single flavor can be a good one, but without other contrasting flavors, it can be one-dimensional, lacking the full taste you want out of your coffee drinking experience.

Just like every step of the process brings out different aspects of potential flavor provided by that specific cultivar or variety, faults and off flavors can come about at various stages of the coffee bean's life, as well. This is important to keep in mind before you rush out to buy that $60 per pound Jamaica Blue Mountain. Just because the cultivar is prized doesn't inherently guarantee its quality; issues with the growing cycle, the processing method, or the roasting can still muck it up. Each of the sections that follow here will explore a step of the process from seed to cup and the potential flavor issues that can arise in each.

Faults from growing

Different cultivars will be at their best at different elevations, rainfall levels, and temperature ranges. The perfect growing conditions for one bean can kill the best potential of another; knowing which beans to plant on which land is one of the first challenges for the coffee farmer.

If a coffee tastes flat or one-dimensional, this can often be the product of faults in the growing process—either a lack of proper nutrients in the soil, a coffee grown at low elevation, or one that didn't receive enough rainfall while it was growing. While coffee trees like heat and humidity, they also don't do well in direct sunlight, preferring the protection of tree canopies in their natural habitat. A coffee that was scorched by too much exposure to the sun can have a flat taste, as well, though it may also have faint carbon or burnt notes, even if it's handled correctly in the roasting and brewing stages. Wide fluctuations in humidity can give the coffee a phenolic flavor, similar to a Band-Aid or burning rubber.

The ripeness of the coffee cherry when it is picked can also have an impact on the flavor. If the cherry was not ripe enough, this could lead to a raw, overly vegetal flavor, similar to a raw peanut or stale grain; you may hear the taste described as "green," which is different than the grassy flavor found in green tea that some find desirable. On the other side of things, if the cherry was allowed to ripen too much on the tree, it can give the coffee a sour flavor, like acetic acid. This may also result in alliaceous notes (like the flavor that comes from garlic or onions).

There are also a variety of pests that like to eat the cherries and leaves of the plants, and these can leave lasting off flavors in the beans. Often the taste will end up being flat and one-dimensional since the beans will be unable to get their proper nutrients as they grow. If the beans have been tainted by the pests, you may find they have a slight turpeny or diesel-like flavor.

Faults from processing

There are multiple stages to the processing of a coffee bean, and multiple accepted methods of completing each stage. Wet-processed beans are removed from their cherries immediately after picking, while dry-processed or natural coffees are allowed to ferment inside the fruits for a designated length of time before being pulped. There are also processes that fall in between these two, called semi-washed or pulped-natural, along with the Monsooned coffee mentioned in the previous chapter. Beyond this comes the question of how the coffee beans are dried after processing. Some are laid out to dry in natural sunlight; others are dried in large mechanical dryers in large batches. Each of the above methods has its own guidelines and correct practices; off flavors often result if these aren't properly followed.

The main off flavors you'll get from problems with the processing will come from the "Fruit Decomposition" section of the Counter Culture off tastes flavor wheel. You can describe these tastes with words like rotten or funky, or by comparing them to tasting like a garbage bin or a compost heap. You may also get a sour note, similar to vinegar or bad wine. Coffees that taste gamey or have notes of animal hide or leather may also have been improperly processed.

Not all of the moisture is removed from a coffee bean during drying. The ideal residual moisture content is between 10% and 12%, depending on the method and the bean. If they're under-dried, this can allow mold to develop within the bean, imparting either phenolic or musty, mildew flavors. If they're over-dried, this most often results in a coffee that tastes flat, losing its complexity, though it can also give the coffee a carbony, scorched taste.

Faults from storage

Once they're processed and dried, green coffee beans can stay fresh for up to a year before they're roasted. They will often sit in a few different warehouses during this time: one at the mill where they were processed, one or more at the importer or distribution centers where they were shipped, and one at the roaster who purchases them. If conditions aren't optimal in any of these places—or during the shipping from one place to the next—you'll taste it in the beans.

Mold growth is perhaps the most common fault picked up during the storage and transportation stage. Depending on the type and severity of the mold growth, this can impart a range of different flavors. It is another potential source of phenolic flavors, although in the case of mold these may be more medicinal or chlorinated than straight burnt rubber. A rotten, iodine-like, decomposing taste is another potential result of mold growth. They may also pick up a musty flavor, a mildewed taste, or a faint taste of raw potato.

Pests can also get into coffee when it's being stored. Both insect and rodent pests are common banes of the coffee warehouse. The off flavors that result from pests at this stage will be similar to the tainted flavors from pests during growing: diesel or turpeny notes, along with a "baggy" flavor or carbony, wood smoke notes.

Even though green coffee lasts a lot longer than roasted coffee, it does still have an expiration date, after which it will begin to go stale. Loss of complexity is one of the most common faults imparted by long storage. The "Aged and faded" section of the off flavor wheel will also come into play; the coffee may take on cardboard or paper notes. It may also have a pronounced woodiness or a taste like stale bread.

Faults from roasting

Over-roasting is a more common issue than under-roasting when it comes to tasting coffee. There are two stages in the roasting process at which the bean splits open to release escaping gasses and steam: the first crack and the second crack. The first crack is an indication that the coffee is roasted enough to brew; coffee removed at this point will be at a light roast level. The second crack happens at the very end of the process, and not all coffees will reach this point. Anything that has roasted to or beyond the second crack will be considered a dark roast.

If coffee is not allowed to reach the first crack before it's removed from the roaster, it will end up having a "green" flavor. This could give it grain-like notes or a vegetal quality, like raw peas. Beans that have reached the second crack (or a temperature of around 450°F) will lose some of their brightness and acidity. These beans are actually preferred by some people, especially as a component of an espresso blend, but won't be ideal for tasting; you'll get mostly roast and dark chocolate flavors. Once a bean passes 500°F, it is officially over-roasted. The flavor notes you'll get from these beans will be almost exclusively from the carbon end of the spectrum, with descriptors like ashy, burnt, or fishy.

Faults from brewing

For tasting, you'll predominantly be using an immersion brew method, so you may not encounter these flavor issues during that process. It's still a good idea to know what problems can arise from the brew, though, especially as you're trying out the coffees you've tasted in other brew methods.

If the coffee was complex during the tasting but flat on another brewing method, it is possible the right amount of hot water was not allowed to make contact with the grounds. A brewing temperature that's too low could result in a sour flavor. An over-extracted brew will often have a chalky or salty feel on the tongue; these could also result from too much water or water that's too hot. A medicinal flavor that gives you a tingling or numbness along the sides of your tongue is also a sign of over-extraction, especially when brewed using the espresso method.

Training Your Palate

It might sound strange to say you need to learn how to taste—after all, eating is one of the only things you've probably been doing your entire life. Being able to identify and name the flavors that are crossing your tongue can be surprisingly tricky, however, especially if you're trying to separate them out from the other bold flavors contained in a cup of coffee.

When you're at the tasting table, your palate will be one of your most useful tools. Learning how to use it correctly can be a time-consuming and tricky process. If the only thing you can think of to say when you taste is that it tastes like coffee, you may need to spend some quality time building up a reference library of tastes, flavors, and sensations that you can use to compare coffee flavors to in the future. Before you can figure out what you're looking for in your perfect cup of coffee, you have to acquire a taste for coffee, in all its subtleties.

Eat mindfully

Studying the flavor wheels mentioned in chapter 3 is one way to build up the right vocabulary to express and describe the tastes you identify in a cup of coffee, but even these helpful aids will be largely meaningless if you don't know what the foods listed on them taste like. Especially when it comes to more subtle differences—say that between a note of lime and a note of lemon—articulating these specific flavors can be tricky if your palate hasn't been trained.

Eating mindfully is simply another way to say that you should pay attention to the tastes and sensations you're experiencing whenever you eat if you're on a mission to train your palate. Pay attention to every aspect of the eating experience, from the initial aroma to the texture and the way it feels on your tongue, along with the more obvious aspects of taste. If you're training your palate specifically for tasting coffee, pay special attention to the ingredients whose flavors are most likely to be part of a coffee's flavor profile—fruits, especially berries and citrus fruits, various varieties of nuts, and baking flavors like cocoa, vanilla, and caramel.

Not everything that can have notes in coffee is something you're probably in the habit of eating by itself. When it comes to things like molasses and maple syrup, picking out those flavors can be tricky if you've never eaten them straight. When it comes to floral notes like jasmine or hibiscus, you can learn them by smell instead of taste. If you detect a certain scent when you walk into a room or walk by a plant, see if you can identify it. You should even pay attention to exactly what makes things taste and smell bad, as well. When you taste or smell something unpleasant, take the time to focus on exactly what you don't like about it; this will be a great benefit in identifying off flavors.

Stay focused

If you're the kind of person who starts every day off with a cup of coffee, you may be so accustomed to the overall profile of the flavor that you can't pick apart the more subtle aspects of the taste. This is the same principle that makes it difficult to detect the odor of the air in your own home unless you've been away for a little while. Being able to effectively taste the notes in coffee means first emptying your mind of these preconceptions, allowing you to get to the true components and roots of the flavor.

Whether you're mindfully tasting another ingredient or sitting down at the tasting table, your first step should always be to empty your mind so that you can focus exclusively on the tastes and sensations on your tongue. Taste is a very fleeting sensation, even more so when you're tasting coffee since the flavor will change as it cools. Make sure you're in the right frame of mind to be able to maintain sharp focus throughout the tasting. This means getting plenty of sleep the night before and drinking plenty of water; your taste buds can react differently when you're dehydrated, and it can also make it more difficult to focus.

Practice makes perfect

Developing a palate that can detect subtle flavors is a skill, and like any skill, it will become more honed with practice. You don't have to be sitting down at an official tasting table to try and pick out notes from your coffee. If you get your beans from a café, they will likely have tasting notes on file that you can look at; if you buy it pre-packaged, these are often on the bag of beans. See how many of these flavor notes you can detect when you're drinking your morning cup—and if you don't get those specific flavors, try to keep track of which flavors you are picking up. Pay attention to the acidity, body, and finish as well as the flavors and aromas.

Remember that taste is a matter of personal preference; there are no right or wrong answers. Whatever you're eating or drinking, pay attention to what tastes you get out of it. To a well-educated palate, telling coffees apart that are from different growing region is as easy as telling the difference between sugar and salt. The more you practice learning the tastes that are in coffee, the larger a collection of descriptors you'll have at your disposal, letting you compare different coffees in a more meaningful way.

Testing your palate

Sometimes it can be difficult to tell just how good your palate is. If you want to test your progress, consider having a friend set up a blind tasting to see if you can distinguish which coffee is which. Have a friend prepare the samples for you without you watching. If you want to truly be tested, ask the friend to buy the coffee, too, so you don't even know what your options are.

The best place to start is to have the samples prepared from coffee at three different roast levels and see if you can determine which one is which by smell and taste alone. Once you can determine a light, medium, and dark roast from each other blind, move on to trying three coffees from different growing regions. Make it easy on yourself at first, and choose one coffee from the Americas, one from Africa, and one from Asia. As you refine your palate, you'll be able to get down to more subtle differences, like determining a Kenya from an Ethiopia, or even between growing regions of the same country.

Professional Cupping

A cupping is the name for the official, controlled tastings that coffee professionals do. These can happen at multiple stages of the coffee life cycle. Owners of a farm will cup the beans from different crops to test them for quality and verify the harvest is yielding the flavors they expect; roasters will cup the coffees when they're deciding which ones to purchase or to combine into blends; and café owners and baristas will cup coffees when they're choosing the right ones to stock on their shelves or use in their drinks.

The idea behind a professional cupping is to remove all possible variables so they can evaluate the coffees on a level playing field. By removing differences in grind, brewing method, and often even in roast level, they're able to evaluate the intrinsic characteristics of the beans, comparing varieties side by side to better make their purchasing decisions. Because of this, professional cuppings will typically have a very stringent protocol in place when it comes to the sequence and timing of events, one that is kept strictly consistent not only within a cupping but across multiple sessions.

There is a fair amount of scientific rigor involved in the process, down to the grading sheets used to evaluate the coffees. The grounds and water are both weighed to a high degree of precision, and the water is often poured using a gooseneck kettle to ensure an even pour. Steps are taken to prevent cross-contamination, not only between different coffees, but between different samples of the same coffee; separate cups and spoons are often used, and the grinder is thoroughly flushed between samples. Professional tasters will also frequently cup blind to avoid having any pre-conceived biases affect their tasting of the coffee.

While a home tasting session can be less rigorously controlled than one done by professionals, understanding the way coffee experts conduct a tasting—and why—will better prepare you to set up one of your own. From the equipment used to how the coffee is sipped, every step of the process is done a certain way for a reason. Though the end goal of most professional cuppings is commercial, the stages involved are all about unlocking the truest flavor of the bean, the same thing you're looking for when you do your own tastings at home.

Setting up

When professionals set up a cupping, they'll often have a station for each sample they're tasting. Each of the samples they will be testing will be weighed out and the whole beans waiting in pre-portioned containers. This allows the coffees to be each ground immediately prior to the brew, rather than wasting time in weighing each sample as you go. This becomes especially important the more coffees you're brewing, to make sure that each sample is being brewed for the proper span of time. Each sample will also have a designated cup into which it is brewed; there may also be a designated spoon for each sample, although there may alternatively be a spoon for each taster, with a glass of water they can use to rinse it between tastings.

Another very important thing that has to be present at any tasting is a spittoon, garbage can, or something else that the coffee can be spit out into. In the same way that sommeliers spit out the wine they're tasting so that they don't get too intoxicated, professional cuppers need to spit out the majority of coffee they drink to avoid becoming over-caffeinated.

Part of the reason professional tasters need to spit out the coffee they taste is the sheer number of coffees they'll be tasting in a session. There can often be slight variations between different beans in the same crop or roasting batch. To account for this—and make sure they're getting a true sense of the coffees that they're drinking—professional cuppers will often do at least three samples of each coffee they're tasting. Depending on how many coffees they're trying out, this could end up being quite a lot to drink in one session.

Brewing

Each sample will use around 12 grams of beans, ground fine immediately prior to brewing. The taster will typically smell the coffee as soon as it comes out of the grinder to get a sense of its aroma. Shaking the grounds will release more of this aroma, letting the taster get a full, hearty whiff. Each sample should be ground separately, with the chute of the grinder cleared completely and the dosing chamber brushed clean between samples to prevent cross-contamination.

Once the coffee is ground, the sample cup should be filled with 5-6 ounces of water just off boiling. The ideal temperature range is the same as other brew methods, between 195°F and 205°F. The water should be poured slowly in concentric circles, ensuring complete saturation of the grounds and looking out for dry clumps on the surface. A gooseneck kettle can be very helpful in controlling the flow of water but is not strictly necessary the way it is for manual brewing methods.

When the water is poured in, some of the grounds will sink to the bottom of the cup, while others will form a crust on the surface. The tasters will examine the crust visually as it's forming, taking note of any changes that occur when the coffee comes into contact with the water. It's also usually a good idea to give the surface a good sniff to get a sense of the aroma and how it's developed.

The coffee should be allowed to brew for around three to four minutes, the same length of time you'd allow for a French press. It may seem strange that such a simple brewing method would be used, with no filter to prevent the grinds from entering the brewed beverage. The reasoning behind this is that it removes any potential influence that more complex brewing methods would have on the coffee. By allowing the water and grinds to maintain direct contact, the full flavor of the bean can be released into the cup. Since the tasters won't be drinking from the cup directly, the grinds that sink to the bottom aren't likely to be stirred up and consumed with the brewed coffee.

This method does mean the surface of the coffee sample will need to be cleaned before the coffee is tasted. To do this, they first take a spoon and break the crust on top by drawing the spoon through the grounds. At this point, the taster should again smell the coffee, taking a deep sniff with his or her nose down close to the surface of the coffee to get the full effect of the aroma, which will be at its peak in this particular moment.

Most of the grounds will settle to the bottom of the cup once the crust is broken. The grounds that stay floating on the surface of the brewed coffee can be scooped off using a spoon and dumped into the spittoon or trash can. This is usually done by taking two designated spoons and placing them at the back of the cup, then bringing them forward around the outer edge in a single, fluid motion. When the spoons meet in the front of the cup, they are scooped up and out, leaving behind as much liquid as possible.

Tasting

Once the surface of the cup has been cleaned, the tasting portion of the cupping is ready to begin. It's a good idea to take a second at this point and forget the aromas that were observed and recorded during the grinding and brewing. The smell of a coffee is directly related to the taste, but each will have its own distinctive nature that a professional taster will try to get a sense of separately.

There is a special technique to tasting like a professional, which is known as "aspirating" the coffee. It is a similar technique to that used by wine tasters to open up the flavor of the wine and reveal all of its complexities on the tongue. A spoonful of coffee is brought up to the taster's lips then sucked violently into their mouth while they take a breath. This technique sprays the coffee over the entire tongue and at the same time draws it into the nasal passages, giving the full array of tastes and aromas. This will make a loud slurping sound if done correctly.

After aspirating, the coffee is moved around on the tongue and through the entire mouth so the taster can get a sense of the mouthfeel as well as the body. Sweetness and acidity are the main points of focus. The taster should note the ways the flavor changes and develops the longer it's in their mouth—whether it gets stronger or flatter, sweeter or softer. Once this step is completed, the coffee is either swallowed or spit out and the aftertaste noted.

This procedure is then repeated with each sample on the table. Every coffee around the table is sampled once, then the taster goes back to taste each coffee again, noting how the flavor has changed as the coffee cools. It is important to note the flavor at various stages of the brew; some characteristics will be easier to discern at a cooler temperature, while others will only come through in the initial taste.

Evaluation

Most professional tasters prefer to stay relatively quiet during the cupping itself. This is both to avoid distractions, maintaining their focus on the flavors themselves, and to prevent having their tastes influenced by the opinions of others at the tasting table. The mind is very susceptible to suggestion; hearing what someone else tasted in a coffee could sway how the other tasters feel about it, as well.

Once everyone has had a chance to get their first impressions of all the coffees, there will often be a sharing of notes and opinions between all the tasters. These results are then written down, with notes taken about the coffee's aroma and flavor, as well as its sweetness, acidity, body, and finish.

In a professional context, many tasters will give the coffee a numerical grade or score once the cupping has concluded. This is traditionally on a scale of 1-100 and corresponds roughly to school grades (90-100 equals an A, 80-89 equals a B, and so on). A numerical score doesn't necessarily need to be given to understand the coffee, however, and many professionals object to this kind of rating system because it reduces the complex combination of flavors in the coffee to a number that ignores the subtleties of the beverage. Regardless of how the evaluation is recorded, however, some kind of record of the tasting experience is key, in both professional and home tasting contexts.

Home Tasting Practices

A home tasting does not need to necessarily follow the same stringent protocols as a professional cupping. Some aspects of a professional cupping—like the grading form filled out at the end, for example—are more confusing than helpful, and often end up being detrimental to the home tasting experience. You should enjoy the coffee tasting, first and foremost. This process is about honing your own skills and finding your perfect cup, not adhering to the standards of a given roaster or coffee shop. Whatever tweaks you have to make to the professional cupping format so it better suits your lifestyle are perfectly acceptable.

Certain aspects of the process do benefit even casual tasters to employ, such as the unique way the coffee samples are brewed. An immersion brewing method is generally the best for bringing out the full flavor potential of the bean because nothing is filtered out. If you'd rather not go through the skimming process described in the previous chapter, a French press will be the best alternative, though it will mean sacrificing the formation and breaking of the crust.

In the same vein, it is a good idea to taste the coffees you make during this process without adding any milk or sugar, even if you would add them to the coffee you drink normally. Anything you add to the coffee is going to change its flavor, obscuring the complex and subtle notes the bean has to offer.

Preplanning

You can do your tastings either alone or in a group. A group setting is often especially beneficial for a beginner because it gives you some people to bounce your ideas off of. Where professional tasters don't often communicate while they're tasting to avoid bias, if you're still training your palate having other people around to tell you what they taste can help you articulate your own discoveries. Keep your mind open to other possibilities, but also don't be afraid to tell people what you taste, even if it's different than what your tasting partners say.

If you are tasting in a group, make sure there are enough samples for everyone; you'll need to make at least two samples of each coffee for a group of four or more. This makes sure everyone isn't trying to crowd their spoon into the same cup, and that everyone gets the experience of cleaning a cup and smelling the aroma released after you break the crust on top.

Once you know how many people you're going to be tasting with, you can buy the right amount of coffee for the session. If you're buying coffees from a variety of countries or regions, try to get coffees that are close to the same roast level. It can also be enjoyable to taste various roast levels of the same region of coffee, if that's an option that's available to you. You can always roast your own green beans at home if you can't find different roast levels of the same coffee in the store. Sampling coffees from the same country but sold by different roasters or coffee shops can also be an interesting experiment, though you will be looking for more subtle variations between them than if you sample coffees with more variety.

Setting up

The first thing you need to figure out is where you're going to do your tasting. Remember that you'll need to have a separate container for each sample of coffee that you make, along with containers to hold the whole beans before you grind them. If there are multiple people participating, make sure they have enough room to move around without bumping into each other. A kitchen is often the ideal location, especially since it also gives you quick access to other tools you'll need, like your kettle and your grinder. Lay out your supplies before you even start weighing out your beans; it'll save you time and stress in the long run.

Organization is important. When you're preparing your samples, label or color-code them so you can tell which is which if they get moved around on the table. Proper organization also means staying consistent with your timing and preparation. All the coffee should ideally be ground to the same degree, use the same coffee to water ratio, be brewed at the same temperature, and have the same brewing time. If there are inconsistencies in your process, you could end up tasting those instead of the differences in the beans.

On the day of the tasting, you want to try and preserve your taste buds as much as possible. Don't eat or drink anything with a particularly strong flavor during the hours before the tasting starts; this holds true during the tasting, as well. If you want to provide snacks, do so after the tasting is over. If you're a smoker, do your best not to smoke immediately before (or during) the tasting, as this can dull both your smell and taste.

The tasting

Look for the characteristics that have been discussed in the previous chapters—not only the notes and tastes, but also the acidity and body. Evaluate how clean the cup is and how much it lingers on your tongue. The taste and length of the aftertaste can be excellent indications of the quality of both the beans and the brew. Feel the weight of the coffee on your tongue and compare its textures to other things you've had to drink. Is it thin like water or tea, or is it creamier, like milk? Whatever you taste, write it down in your tasting journal. Have notebooks or sheets of paper for the other members of the group to do the same.

It can be easy to wear out your palate during a coffee tasting. The flavors in coffee are so strong that they can easily overwhelm your taste buds if you drink too many in a row. Flushing your mouth out with water between coffees can help. You can also keep unsalted soda crackers at the table to nibble on between samples as a palate cleanser.

Whatever variations you make to the tasting process, remember that consistency is the golden rule. Do the same thing with each sample, and preferably the same thing every time you taste. As you continue to perfect your technique and hone your palate, you'll be able to pick out ever more subtle notes of the coffee, expanding the value of the tasting in your life.

The Full Picture

It can be argued that coffee tasting is even more important for finding quality versions of the beverage than it is for wine. When you buy a bottle of wine, it will be labeled with a wealth of information—the type of grape, the year it was bottled, and the region it grew it. Finding exceptional wines can sometimes be more about memorizing the ideal characteristics outlined by other than it is about finding those high-quality offerings yourself.

A bag of coffee will not give you such a comprehensive picture of the contents. It will be labeled with the country of origin, and typically the roast level; if you're lucky, you may also get the name of the region or the cultivar. Not only is this not enough information to truly give you a picture of the coffee's flavor, there is more variation in coffee than there is in wine. Changes to the climate during the harvest season can completely alter the character of the bean; changes in the processing, storage, and roasting can be equally impactful.

Coffee professionals have to be more active in their selection process than sommeliers. New cultivars are frequently being produced or tried in locations where they haven't been grown before. As the world's climate continues to shift, areas that were once prized for their excellent beans have become less consistent, and vice versa. When it comes to the world of coffee, there is always something new to be discovered.

Deep understanding of coffee flavors is often best achieved through comparison. By lining up several coffees side by side, you'll be able to note the differences and similarities better than you could by tasting a single coffee in a vacuum. The more coffees you taste, the more points of comparison you'll have for the next, and the better you'll be able to pick out the beverage's distinctive notes. Learning the terminology will help to speak more knowledgeably about the things you're tasting, but there is really no shortcut to developing a strong palate. Doing so requires a lot of time and practice. The good news is that practice can be both fun and rewarding, opening you up to the full range of flavors that high-quality coffee has to offer.

Win a free

kindle
OASIS

Let us know what you thought of this book to enter the sweepstake at:

http://booksfor.review/coffee

Also Available by **Jessica Simms**

Steaming Milk

Also Available by **Jessica Simms**

Making Crema

Making Crema

The Art and Science of the Perfect Espresso Shot

JESSICA SIMMS

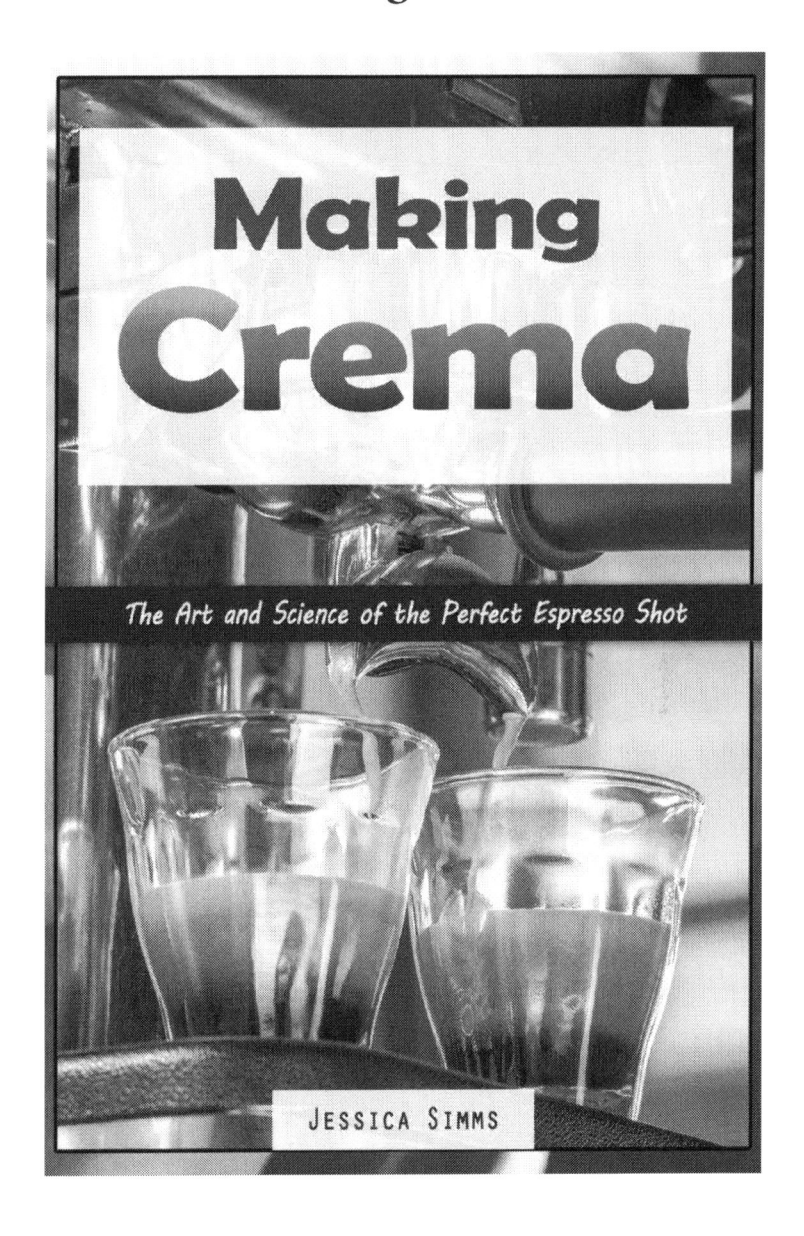

Printed in Great Britain
by Amazon